The Australian To
194

Peter Griffiths
and
Peter Wynne-Thomas

LIMLOW
BOOKS

First published in Great Britain by
Limlow Books Limited
St. Peter's Hill, Litlington, Royston SG8 0QF
1992

British Library Cataloguing-in-Publication Data
A catalogue record for this book is available from the British Library.

ISBN 1 874524 01 7

Printed by Peartree Printers, Derby

Introduction

The Australian tour of 1948 was, of course, recorded in *Wisden*. However, as was the prevailing custom, details of the scorecards which are now considered essential were not included. This work is intended to bring together all of those details - captains and wicketkeepers, close of play scores, fall of wickets, second innings batting order and which bowlers bowled the no-balls and wides. The Australians, throughout the summer, scored their runs at a phenomenal rate, and we have, thanks to Ray Webster, included duration of innings, where available.

We would like to thank several people for their help in the compilation of this book. Ray Webster checked the scorecards and gave us much extra information. Chris Harte supplied information on the matches played in Australia. S.S.Perera sent us the details of the match played in Colombo. Tim Walton also supplied missing details. Our thanks also go to Bob Jones for lending the team photograph.

* against a player indicates the captain.
† against a player indicates the wicketkeeper.
† against a team name indicates that the match was not first-class.

Peter Griffiths
Peter Wynne-Thomas
October 1992

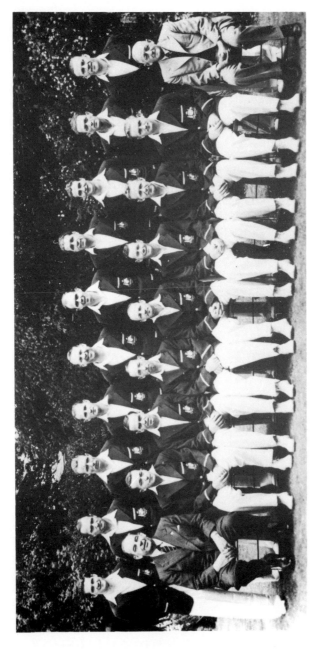

The Australian Touring Team 1948

R.N.Harvey, S.G.Barnes, R.R.Lindwall, R.A.Saggers, D.T.Ring, W.A.Johnston, E.R.H.Toshack, K.R.Miller, D.Tallon, S.J.E.Loxton

K.O.E.Johnson, R.A.Hamence, I.W.Johnson, A.L.Hassett, D.G.Bradman, W.A.Brown, A.R.Morris, C.L.McCool, W.Ferguson
(Manager)   (Captain)   (Scorer)

The Background to The Tour

The last official visit to England by an Australian team had been in 1938, when each side had won a Test, two others had been drawn and the match at Old Trafford totally washed out. The Australian bowling had been weak, only O'Reilly being a consistent match winner: the batting, dominated by Bradman, strong. The margin between England and Australia had been slight, but Australia retained the Ashes, which they had recaptured in 1934.

As soon as the war in Europe ceased in May 1945, a series of 'Victory' Tests was staged between the Combined Australian Forces in England and the available strength of England. The only Test player on the Australian side was Hassett, though the outstanding member of the team was Keith Miller, who had made his first-class debut for Victoria in 1937/38. The series of five matches ended two each and one draw.

With the cessation of hostilities in the Far East, the Australian Board of Control issued an invitation to M.C.C. to send a team to Australia as soon as practical. The season of 1946/47 was agreed upon. England lost the series by three matches to nil, with two drawn.

The reasons behind England's defeat, or Australia's victory, were written down as 'bad luck' (England seemed to have the worst of weather conditions in which to play vital innings), bad umpiring (a cause that was not really convincing), bad captaincy (Hammond however was surely no better or worse than he had been in 1938). The plain truth was that Australia had unearthed two brilliant bowlers in Lindwall and Miller, together with excellent back-up in the guise of Toshack, Tribe, Johnson, Dooland etc. They had totally discarded their pre-war attack, but still retained in Bradman, Barnes, Hassett and Brown their major batsmen. The single post-war bowler of consequence in the England 1946/47 camp was Bedser. The only other really notable post-war England discovery was Evans.

Could England make up the leeway by 1948? This was the question asked. A study of the 1947 English season averages supplies the answer. Gladwin, Laker and Cook of the younger generation had good summers among the bowlers, Cranston and Tremlett as all-rounders and Simpson as one of several batsmen. All useful players but they hardly compared with the Australian discoveries, especially as Harvey and Johnston were added to the list in 1947/48.

The Australians were therefore the favourites to win the 1948 series.

The Australian Touring Party

D.G.Bradman (*South Australia*). Aged 39.
Previously toured in 1930, 1934 and 1938.
As the world's outstanding batsman there was no question of his place in the side on his ability, but in September 1947 there were some doubts expressed as to whether he would agree to tour. During the war he had suffered ill-health and though he played in the 1946/47 series against England he was clearly not the batsman he had been in 1938. Bradman was however one of the three selectors chosen for the 1947/48 series v India and for the touring party itself. Whether he went to England in 1948 appeared to depend on his form against India in 1947/48. He had been Australia's captain since the 1936/37 series v England. If he toured it would be as captain. Bradman was outstandingly successful against the 1947/48 Indians, though he only turned out in one Sheffield Shield game, scoring 100 v Victoria in his single innings. As Bradman's success in the Tests v India unfolded, it was obvious that he would make a final tour to England.

A.L.Hassett (*Victoria*). Aged 34.
Previously toured in 1938 and captained the 1945 Services Team.
A natural stroke making batsman, who was nimble on his feet, Hassett played with success in both the 1946/47 and 1947/48 Test series and in the latter season had topped the Victorian batting averages. He was captain of his state and therefore the most appropriate man as vice-captain of the 1948 tourists. His experience and form made him an automatic choice for the side.

W.A.Brown (*Queensland*). Aged 35.
Previously toured in 1934 and 1938.
A stylish opening batsman who possessed plenty of patience, Brown had missed virtually the whole of the 1946/47 season due to a thumb injury. He returned as captain of Queensland in 1947/48 heading the Queensland batting table, though having only five completed innings. He regained his Test place and fortunately for him hit 99 in the Fifth Test against India, just before the touring team was selected.

S.G.Barnes (*New South Wales*). Aged 31.
Previously toured in 1938.
An unconventional figure, he missed half of the 1938 tour due to injury, but made a brilliant 234 in the Second Test of 1946/47. He made another Test hundred in the 1947/48 series as well as being the leading New South Wales batsman for the season. The choice of an opening partner for Morris lay between Barnes and Brown. Barnes' reputation as a fieldsman at very close short leg was already well known.

K.R.Miller (*New South Wales*). Aged 28.
Member of the 1945 Australian Services Team.
He was the most exciting batsman in Australia, as well as the leading all-rounder. The point was made that if his fast bowling was over-used his batting would suffer. He came second in both batting and bowling averages for the 1946/47 Test series, but was not quite so successful during the 1947/48 season either in Tests or Sheffield Shield.

A.R.Morris (*New South Wales*). Aged 26.
A left-handed opening batsman, he scored a century in each innings on his debut for New South Wales in 1940/41 and hit three hundreds against England in the 1946/47 series. He was not so successful against India in 1947/48, though hitting 100 in the Third Test. His footwork was perhaps his weak point.

R.R.Lindwall (*New South Wales*). Aged 26.
He was regarded as the fastest bowler in the side, possessing an ideal fast bowler's run up and delivery, though the dragging of his right toe caused some adverse comments. He took most wickets in both the 1946/47 and 1947/48 Test series and in combination with Miller provided Australia with the most fearsome new ball attack in the world. He had a Test 100 to his name and was a very useful man to have coming in at number 8.

C.L.McCool (*Queensland*). Aged 32.
A talented all-rounder, being a right-hand middle order batsman and a leg-break bowler, who flights the ball, he had an excellent record in the 1946/47 series, but was nothing like as prominent in the 1947/48 season. He could find problems adapting his bowling to English conditions.

E.R.H.Toshack (*New South Wales*). Aged 33.
A left-arm medium pace bowler, he was expected to be the workhorse of the side, though a knee injury caused him problems in 1947/48 and would place some doubts on his ability to survive a full English summer. He usually bowled over the wicket to a leg-side field and could move the ball either way. He played in all five 1946/47 Tests and but for injury would have done so again in 1947/48.

I.W.Johnson (*Victoria*). Aged 29.
The principal off-break bowler in the side, he played with some success in four Tests both in 1946/47 and 1947/48 despite the fact that off-break bowlers were regarded as the least effective type of bowler in Australia. He had the technique to score runs, though he made very few in 1947/48.

W.A.Johnston (*Victoria*). Aged 26.
A tall left-arm fast medium bowler he made the ball lift awkwardly on a receptive pitch. Johnston could also bowl usefully at a slower pace. He was very successful against India in 1947/48, his 16 wickets costing 11 runs each.

D.Tallon (*Queensland*). Aged 32.
He was considered by the 1947/48 Indian tourists as the world's best wicketkeeper, but, though he made his first-class debut in 1933/34, he did not play for Australia until after the War. He had appeared in all eleven Australian post-war Tests and was an automatic choice for the tour. Tallon was also a useful lower order batsman.

R.A.Saggers (*New South Wales*). Aged 30.
Chosen as reserve wicketkeeper, Saggers had not played in Test cricket, but was clearly the preferred understudy for Tallon. He was also a useful batsman.

D.T.Ring (*Victoria*). Aged 29.
A leg-break and googly bowler who tended to deliver the ball with more speed than his rivals, his first Test for Australia was the Fifth and final game of 1947/48, when he took six wickets. His change of pace could bring him many wickets in England. He was not noted as a batsman.

R.N.Harvey (*Victoria*). Aged 19.
Described as the most gifted teenage cricketer since Miller made his debut, Harvey was a left-hand batsman, with vast natural ability. The youngest member of the touring party he made his Test debut v India in 1947/48 and in his second game hit 153. He was one of six cricketing brothers, four of whom played first-class cricket. In addition to his batting he was an outstanding cover field.

S.J.E.Loxton (*Victoria*). Aged 27.
A fast medium bowler and forceful middle order batsman, Loxton scored 80 on his Test debut - the final game against the 1947/48 Indians. His record for Victoria however in the same season was not all that impressive, though in his first summer he had shot to fame with 232 against Queensland.

R.A.Hamence (*South Australia*). Aged 32.
A right-hand batsman he played in one Test against England in 1946/47 and two against India in 1947/48, but achieved little. However for South Australia he twice hit two separate hundreds in a match. He might be considered the luckiest player to have been chosen for the tour.

K.O.E.Johnson (*Manager*). Aged 53.
A Flight-Lieutenant in the RAAF during the War, he was employed doing public relations work in London in the spring of 1945 and then found himself manager of the Australian Services Team which played during the summer. His knowledge of the English cricket scene therefore made him a natural choice as the backroom man of the tour.

Eighteen cricketers had taken part in the Test series of 1947/48 against India and two of these could be considered most unlucky not to have been included in the party for England: Bruce Dooland (South Australia), aged 24 - he was a leg-break and googly bowler as well as a very useful batsman; Leonard Johnson (Queensland), aged 28 - a medium pace bowler and hard hitting batsman. Others who were mentioned as possibilities included J.Pettiford (New South Wales), F.W.Freer (Victoria), M.R.Harvey (Victoria), brother of Neil, and K.D.Meuleman (Victoria).

England's Test Cricketers 1948

The Test Match selection committee of A.J.Holmes (chairman), J.C.Clay and R.W.V.Robins with the captain co-opted chose the following 22 players during the summer.

N.W.D.Yardley (*Yorkshire*). Aged 33.
A middle order batsman and medium pace change bowler, Yardley had made his Test debut on the 1938/39 tour to South Africa and had been the vice-captain of the 1946/47 tour to Australia. In 1947 he had led England in all five Tests, but like many other Test players had declined to tour the West Indies in 1947/48. There had been some suggestion that R.W.V.Robins might be chosen as England's captain, but as he resigned as Middlesex captain at the end of 1947, this was hardly a serious suggestion. Yardley therefore was the sole candidate as England's captain.

L.Hutton (*Yorkshire*). Aged 31.
The outstanding opening batsman of the era, he had topped the Test batting averages on the 1946/47 tour to Australia and though eclipsed by Edrich and Compton in the 1947 series against South Africa, Hutton had performed well. In 1947/48 he had gone out as a late reinforcement to the injured England team in the West Indies and again performed well. He was an automatic choice for the First Test.

C.Washbrook (*Lancashire*). Aged 33.
He established himself as Hutton's opening partner in the 'Victory' Tests of 1945 and had an excellent tour of Australia in 1946/47. He did not go to the West Indies in 1947/48, but there was no doubt about Washbrook being chosen for the Trent Bridge Test of 1948.

W.J.Edrich (*Middlesex*). Aged 32.
Edrich had a rather chequered Test career until the 1946/47 Australian tour, when he performed brilliantly. This form was even more enhanced in 1947. He did not tour the West Indies in 1947/48, but was another automatic choice for the First Test of 1948. Apart from his determined batting, his fast bowling was a considerable asset, as England were acutely short of bowlers capable of worrying the Australians.

D.C.S.Compton (*Middlesex*). Aged 29.
Establishing himself in the Middlesex side of 1936, his batting talent was such that the following summer he had gained an England place and effectively had at once secured a permanent position in Test cricket. He had broken all records in 1947 and though not touring the West Indies in 1947/48, was another automatic choice for 1948.

J.Hardstaff (*Nottinghamshire*). Aged 36.
With the first four batting places occupied by certainties, Hardstaff was one of several contenders for the fifth place. His batting in 1947, allied to his success in the West Indies in 1947/48 and his hundred for Notts v Australians early in the tour, made him the favoured candidate. A very stylish batsman, he had been an automatic choice for England in the period 1936 to 1939, but had not commanded a regular Test place since 1946.

C.J.Barnett (*Gloucestershire*). Aged 37.
He was a very controversial choice for the First Test. He had played in three Tests in 1947, but with limited success. Barnett did not go on either the 1946/47 or the 1947/48 tour. His ability to bowl played a part in his selection, but it seemed optimistic of the selectors to expect Barnett's bowling to worry the Australians.

T.G.Evans (*Kent*). Aged 27.
With the resumption of first-class cricket in 1946, it did not take long for Evans to establish himself as England's principal wicketkeeper. He was clearly a class above Gibb and Griffith, the two rivals in 1946 and 1947. He was a great success in Australia in 1946/47, and one of the few automatic choices for England who went on the tour to the West Indies in 1947/48. In addition to his keeping he was a very useful lower order batsman.

J.C.Laker (*Surrey*). Aged 26.
Although he topped the Surrey bowling table of 1947, he was not among the off-spinners chosen for the Tests of that summer. However he went to the West Indies in the winter and was the single success among the young uncapped players in the party. As such he deserved a chance in the First Test.

A.V.Bedser (*Surrey*). Aged 29.
Chosen for the 1946 Tests against India, Bedser quickly showed his ability as a medium fast bowler and was from that point on the one member of the England bowling line-up to perform consistently well. He was the single bowler to be regarded as an automatic choice.

J.A.Young (*Middlesex*). Aged 35.
A slow left-arm bowler who had played for Middlesex since 1933, he had never toured abroad with a major English team and his single Test had been the Fourth v South Africa in 1947. Young had the best record in the 1947 season among left-arm spinners in county cricket. Wardle, the Yorkshire left-armer had gone on the 1947/48 tour to the West Indies, but had done nothing there to promote his Test career.

R.T.Simpson (*Nottinghamshire*). Aged 28.
An attractive middle order right-hand batsman, he had made many runs in wartime cricket until posted overseas. He had a good batting summer in 1947 and two good innings for Notts v Australians early in 1948 were likely to earn him a place in the squad for the First Test.

D.V.P.Wright (*Kent*). Aged 33.
A regular choice for England, he was unable to play in the First Test due to illness, but gained selection for the Second. Unique among English county bowlers, he sent down medium pace leg-breaks. On his day he could be deadly, but he was also prone to periods of erratic deliveries, conceding many runs. He only appeared in one Test in 1948.

H.E.Dollery (*Warwickshire*). Aged 33.
On the strength of some excellent batting in county cricket in 1946, he gained a place in the First Test of 1947, but did not come off. Given a second chance in 1948, he again achieved little.

A.Coxon (*Yorkshire*). aged 32.
Brought in for the Second Test as Bedser's opening partner, Coxon had a good record as a fast medium bowler for Yorkshire, but did little on his Test debut and was not again selected.

G.M.Emmett (*Gloucestershire*). Aged 35.
A very competent opening batsman for his county, he was called upon to replace Hutton in the Third 1948 Test, having never before represented England or toured with M.C.C. He was out of his depth against the Australian attack and this match proved to be his only cap for England.

J.F.Crapp (*Gloucestershire*). Aged 35.
A sound left-hand middle order batsman he scored prolifically for his county in the immediate post-war years. Selected for the Third 1948 Test he retained his place for the remaining two games and then went with M.C.C. to South Africa in 1948/49.

R.Pollard (*Lancashire*). Aged 36.
A fast medium bowler, Pollard had been very successful in the Second Test of 1946 against India. This had led to his selection for the tour to Australia in 1946/47, but he did not play in any of the Tests and did not appear for England in 1947. He played in two of the 1948 matches, being as unsuccessful as the other bowlers who partnered Bedser.

K.Cranston (*Lancashire*). Aged 30.
A useful all-rounder and captain of Lancashire, Cranston had played in three Tests in 1947 and achieved useful performances. He was then appointed vice-captain of the M.C.C. side to the West Indies the following winter. In very difficult circumstances he not only captained England in one Test, but was the tour's best all-rounder. He played in the Fourth Test of 1948, but the Australians were really too good for him.

J.G.Dewes (*Cambridge University and Middlesex*). Aged 21.
He was the opening left-hand batsman for Cambridge and had an excellent summer at Fenner's. To choose him in place of Washbrook for the Fifth Test of 1948 seemed a very bold move by the selectors. Miller and Lindwall showed that Dewes still had a lot to learn.

A.J.Watkins (*Glamorgan*). Aged 26.
Left-handed both as a batsman and medium fast bowler, Watkins was a member of the Glamorgan side which was threatening to win the County Championship, when he was chosen for the Fifth Test. It was another bold move by the selectors, but did not come off. Watkins was far too inexperienced in top class cricket at this stage of his career.

W.E.Hollies (*Warwickshire*). Aged 36.
A long established leg-spin bowler, Hollies had played in three Tests in 1947. He was at the time of his selection for the Fifth Test the leading leg-break bowler of the season and had bowled particularly well for Warwickshire against the Australians. He was the only English bowler to come out of the last Test with any credit.

TASMANIA v AUSTRALIAN XI†

Played at Hobart on March 5, 6 1948
Match drawn
Toss won by Tasmania

Having won the toss Morrisby opened with Thomas but was bowled leg stump second ball. The 58 put on for the second wicket was the best partnership of the innings, the rest falling quickly. The Australians attacked the bowling, the first 100 taking only 71 minutes and Tasmania's score being passed in 81 minutes.

On the second day, Harvey, Loxton and Lindwall all scored heavily before lunch, adding 219 in the session before the declaration. The Tasmanians managed to hold out, the Australian XI bowling being accurate but not especially hostile.

TASMANIA v AUSTRALIAN XI†

Tasmania

R.O.G.Morrisby*	b Lindwall	0	run out		55
R.V.Thomas	c Saggers b Loxton	23	c Barnes b Loxton		34
W.T.Walmsley	c Bradman b Ring	34	not out		41
M.R.Thomas	c Barnes b Ring	17	run out		0
E.E.Rodwell	b Lindwall	0	c and b Johnson		18
A.E.Wilkes	b Lindwall	0	b Loxton		12
J.F.L.Laver	run out	6	c Johnson b Loxton		2
C.G.Richardson	b Johnson	5	c Hassett b Morris		11
N.V.Diprose	c Harvey b Ring	9	not out		2
L.J.Alexander†	not out	12			
I.T.Clay	c Johnston b Ring	10			
Extras	lb 4, nb 2	6	b 6, lb 5		11
Total		122	7 wkts		186

Fall of wickets (1): 1-0, 2-58, 3-68, 4-68, 5-75, 6-75, 7-86, 8-100, 9-100, 10-122
Fall of wickets (2): 1-69, 2-111, 3-113, 4-144, 5-164, 6-166, 7-182

Australian XI

S.G.Barnes	hit wkt b Clay	111
A.R.Morris	c Morrisby b Richardson	33
D.G.Bradman*	c M.R.Thomas b Walmsley	45
A.L.Hassett	b Richardson	100
R.N.Harvey	c Alexander b Rodwell	104
S.J.E.Loxton	not out	66
R.R.Lindwall	not out	65
I.W.Johnson	did not bat	
R.A.Saggers†	did not bat	
W.A.Johnston	did not bat	
D.T.Ring	did not bat	
Extras	b 10, lb 2, nb 2	14
Total	5 wkts dec.	538

Fall of wickets: 1-65, 2-124, 3-283, 4-303, 5-450

Australian XI Bowling

	O	M	R	W		O	M	R	W
Lindwall	8	0	20	3	(2nb)	7	1	24	0
Johnston	5	2	19	1		10	1	25	0
Johnson	4	0	23	0		11	3	28	1
Loxton	4	0	18	1		9	1	22	3
Ring	6.2	0	36	4		13	1	66	0
Barnes						4	2	4	0
Morris						4	2	6	1

Tasmania Bowling

	O	M	R	W	
Richardson	19	0	122	2	
Rodwell	11	0	67	1	
Clay	16	0	88	1	(2nb)
Walmsley	11	0	103	1	
Diprose	13	0	84	0	
Laver	5	0	60	0	

Umpires: A.J.Watkins and W.Lonergan
Close of play: Australian XI 319-4 (Harvey 17, Loxton 10)

S.G.Barnes scored 111 in 176 minuntes. A.L.Hassett scored 100 in 76 minutes with 1 six and 11 fours.
R.N.Harvey scored 104 in 89 minutes with 2 sixes and 11 fours. M.R.Thomas was struck in the mouth by a ball
from Lindwall in the Tasmania first innings and retired hurt at 68-3.

TASMANIA v AUSTRALIAN XI†

Played at Launceston on March 8, 9 1948
Australian XI won by an innings and 49 runs
Toss won by Tasmania

Hamence was picked for the match but withdrew with malaria, being replaced by Brown. Toshack bowling with a gale-force wind behind him and to a leg-side field returned 5-24, the Tasmanian side again being bowled out cheaply. Brown and Morris put on a century opening partnership to quickly overtake the Tasmania total.

On the second morning, Ivor Clay claimed 5-25 to clean up the Australian XI innings. His figures could have been better - he also had Johnston dropped. The Tasmania second innings lasted for less than two hours - a good scoring rate - but wickets fell regularly. Barnes finished off the match with 3 wickets for 1 run.

TASMANIA v AUSTRALIAN XI†

Tasmania

R.O.G.Morrisby*	b Miller	10	run out		7
R.V.Thomas	c Loxton b Toshack	20	lbw b Johnston		1
W.T.Walmsley	lbw b Toshack	17	b Miller		4
M.R.Thomas	lbw b Toshack	4	b Toshack		14
E.E.Rodwell	c Miller b McCool	22	c Saggers b McCool		28
A.Shepherd	c Morris b Toshack	2	(8) c Saggers b Barnes		8
J.F.L.Laver	b Johnston	16	b McCool		8
C.G.Richardson	c Johnston b Toshack	18	(6) c Brown b McCool		22
N.V.Diprose	b Johnston	5	not out		21
L.J.Alexander†	run out	0	b Barnes		0
I.T.Clay	not out	3	c Miller b Barnes		0
Extras	b 3, lb 2, nb 1	6	b 2, lb 1		3
Total		123			116

Fall of wickets (1): 1-10, 2-43, 3-54, 4-69, 5-78, 6-84, 7-100, 8-112, 9-112, 10-123
Fall of wickets (2): 1-4, 2-12, 3-12, 4-41, 5-65, 6-81, 7-94, 8-104, 9-104, 10-116

Australian XI

W.A.Brown	c Walmsley b Diprose	66
A.R.Morris	c Morrisby b Walmsley	61
K.R.Miller	c Richardson b Laver	16
R.N.Harvey	c R.V.Thomas b Walmsley	1
S.J.E.Loxton	c Alexander b Clay	54
C.L.McCool	b Clay	32
S.G.Barnes	c M.R.Thomas b Clay	11
A.L.Hasset*	c Rodwell b Clay	23
R.A.Saggers†	not out	6
E.R.H.Toshack	c Alexander b Clay	0
W.A.Johnston	c Laver b Diprose	10
Extras	lb 8	8
Total		288

Fall of wickets: 1-127, 2-129, 3-130, 4-158, 5-233, 6-242, 7-254, 8-275, 9-275, 10-288

Australian XI Bowling

	O	M	R	W		O	M	R	W
Miller	5	0	13	1	(1nb)	5	0	24	1
Johnston	10	2	28	2		3	0	7	1
McCool	11	1	49	1		12	0	42	3
Toshack	10.2	3	24	5		7	0	30	1
Loxton	3	1	3	0		2	0	9	0
Barnes						1.2	1	1	3

Tasmania Bowling

	O	M	R	W
Clay	15	0	63	5
Richardson	10	0	50	0
Diprose	14.6	0	56	2
Rodwell	3	0	12	0
Walmsley	13	0	68	2
Laver	6	2	31	1

Umpires: R.J.Harrison and C.Thomas
Close of play: Australian XI 223-4 (Loxton 48, McCool 27)

W.A.Brown and A.R.Morris added 127 for the 1st wicket.

WESTERN AUSTRALIA v AUSTRALIAN XI

Played at Perth on March 13, 15, 16 1948
Match drawn
Toss won by Western Australia

Western Australia batted steadily all of the first day, Langdon's innings being the highlight. When B.A.Rigg had scored 5, he was struck on the arm by a ball from Miller and retired hurt with the score at 149-5. He resumed at the fall of the seventh wicket.

Both Morris and Bradman made very attractive centuries on the second day. C.W.Puckett was struck on the leg by a drive from Bradman and sustained a burst blood vessel which prevented him from taking any further part in the match. A.W.Dick substituted on the second day and L.H.Bandy on the third day.

The Australian XI batted rapidly before lunch on the final day and then more steadily until the declaration at tea. The Western Australia innings started in poor light which gradually grew worse. They finally appealed against the light and the match ended, as it had looked like doing for most of the day, in a tame draw.

WESTERN AUSTRALIA v AUSTRALIAN XI

Western Australia

D.K.Carmody*	c Saggers b Johnson	15	b Miller		5
A.R.Edwards	c Brown b Miller	57	not out		21
T.M.Outridge	c Saggers b Miller	9	b McCool		22
M.U.Herbert	c and b Johnston	1			
A.D.Watt	b Johnston	32	not out		1
C.W.Langdon	b McCool	112			
B.A.Rigg	c Johnson b Toshack	65	(4) b Johnson		6
G.T.Kessey †	lbw b Toshack	3			
T.E.O'Dwyer	c Miller b Johnson	31			
C.W.Puckett	b McCool	14			
K.R.Cumming	not out	3			
Extras	b 4, lb 1, w 1	6	b 6, lb 1		7
Total	(356 mins)	348	(65 mins)	3 wkts	62

Fall of wickets (1): 1-36, 2-73, 3-82, 4-87, 5-138, 6-157, 7-228, 8-286, 9-342, 10-348
Fall of wickets (2): 1-6, 2-43, 3-60

Australian XI

W.A.Brown	c Cumming b Rigg	9
A.R.Morris	c sub (A.W.Dick) b Langdon	115
D.G.Bradman*	c Outridge b O'Dwyer	115
K.R.Miller	c Kessey b Watt	43
R.N.Harvey	run out	79
R.A.Hamence	not out	33
C.L.McCool	c Watt b O'Dwyer	18
I.W.Johnson	c sub (A.W.Dick) b O'Dwyer	11
R.A.Saggers†	not out	0
W.A.Johnston	did not bat	
E.R.H.Toshack	did not bat	
Extras	b 12, lb 7	19
Total	(417 mins) 7 wkts dec.	442

Fall of wickets: 1-48, 2-249, 3-255, 4-367, 5-383, 6-416, 7-436

Australian XI Bowling

	O	M	R	W		O	M	R	W
Miller	18	6	36	2	(1w)	3	0	12	1
Johnston	21	3	57	2		4	0	14	0
Toshack	23	2	62	2					
Johnson	20	3	72	2		6	2	9	1
McCool	18.7	1	115	2		5	0	20	1

Western Australia Bowling

	O	M	R	W
Cumming	29	9	60	0
Puckett	15.4	5	19	0
Rigg	7	0	65	1
O'Dwyer	23	4	99	3
Herbert	27	3	127	0
Watt	8	1	36	1
Langdon	5	0	17	1

Umpires: J.P.Robbins and E.T.Tonkinson
Close of play: 1st day: Western Australia (1) 289-8 (Rigg 21, Puckett 2); 2nd day: Australian XI (1) 257-3 (Miller 0, Harvey 0)

C.W.Langdon scored 112 in 188 minutes with 16 fours. A.R.Morris scored 115 in 214 minutes with 14 fours. D.G.Bradman scored 115 in 141 minutes with 16 fours. A.R.Morris and D.G.Bradman added 201 in 141 minutes for the 2nd wicket. K.R.Miller and R.N.Harvey added 112 in 118 minutes for the 4th wicket.

CEYLON v AUSTRALIAN XI†

Played at Colombo on March 27 1948
Match drawn
Toss won by Australian XI

It was estimated that a record 20,000 spectators came to watch this one day game. The Australians won the toss and decided to bat, but Coomaraswamy and Allen, keeping an accurate length, never allowed the early batsmen much freedom. The brightest batting came from Miller, in the afternoon, the score at lunch having been 93 for two. Miller was eventually caught in the deep for 46, with a six and three fours. Loxton also hit a six and was then caught in the outfield.

Rain interrupted play and tea was taken. Ceylon had 19.2 overs batting, then the rain returned and ended the match at 5.15.

The Australians re-embarked at 9.00 that evening and an hour later the S.S.Strathaird sailed out of Colombo.

CEYLON v AUSTRALIAN XI†

Australian XI

S.G.Barnes	retired ill	49
W.A.Brown	lbw b Coomaraswamy	3
D.G.Bradman*	c de Kretser b Heyn	20
K.R.Miller	c Gunasekera b de Kretser	46
R.N.Harvey	c Jayawickrema b Coomaraswamy	8
R.A.Hamence	b Coomaraswamy	0
S.J.E.Loxton	c Rodrigo b de Kretser	34
R.A.Saggers†	b Coomaraswamy	6
I.W.Johnson	not out	2
D.T.Ring	not out	6
E.R.H.Toshack	did not bat	
Extras		10
Total	7 wkts dec.	184

Fall of wickets: 1-8, 2-68, 3-86, 4-106, 5-106, 6-144, 7-173, 8-178

Ceylon

S.Nagendra	lbw b Barnes	5
M.Rodrigo	c and b Johnson	26
F.C.De Saram	not out	7
M.Sathasivam*	not out	6
S.S.Jayawickrema		
B.R.Heyn		
C.I.Gunasekera		
S.Coomaraswamy		
C.Allen		
R.L.de Kretser		
B.Navaratne†		
Extras		2
Total	2 wkts	46

Fall of wickets: 1-13, 2-38

Ceylon Bowling

	O	M	R	W
Allen	13.1	2	33	0
Coomaraswamy	15	2	45	4
Heyn	15	0	43	1
Jayawickrema	5	1	14	0
de Kretser	12	1	39	2

Australian XI Bowling

	O	M	R	W
Miller	2	1	3	0
Loxton	2	1	3	0
Johnson	3	2	6	1
Ring	4.2	1	10	0
Toshack	4	1	16	0
Barnes	4	1	6	1

Umpires: H.E.W.de Zilwa and D.S.Soysa

Note that contemporary accounts give the Australian innings as 8 wickets declared, but definitely give Barnes as retired ill.

WORCESTERSHIRE v AUSTRALIANS

Played at Worcester on April 28, 29, 30 1948
Australians won by an innings and 17 runs
Toss won by Worcestershire

The discussions prior to the game centered on two points, first whether Lindwall would be no-balled for dragging and second whether Bradman would equal his double hundreds of the three previous visits. Neither in fact occurred. The umpires allowed Lindwall's drag and Bradman satisfied himself with 107, then threw away his wicket. The match began in chilly conditions with rain in the air. Kenyon was dismissed second ball of the match; the schoolmaster, C.H.Palmer, survived the opening attack and used his feet to the spinners. His innings, in retrospect, was regarded as one of the best against the Australians during the tour. His fifty came in 50 minutes and he hit thirteen fours and a six. By the close the tourists were 10 without loss.

On the second day it was a race between Morris and Bradman for the first Australian hundred. Bradman reached 99, Morris was on 98, the latter however had the strike and took the honour. Bradman's innings was dominated by some superb drives; he batted two and a quarter hours with fifteen fours. Morris had been uncertain in the early part of his innings, then gradually settled to the strange conditions.

The Australians were 337 for six overnight. On the third morning, Bradman allowed the innings to continue and Miller took the opportunity to hit a bright 50. The off-spinner Jackson earned his six wickets. The features of Worcestershire's second innings were some more good batting by Palmer and a fifty from the Ceylonese cricketer, Outschoorn. The Australian attack was mainly spin. R.E.S.Wyatt, the old England cricketer, was unable to bat in the second innings owing to 'flu. McCool exploited the worn pitch and in a spell of 14 overs took four wickets for 15 runs. An estimated 32,000 attended during the three days and receipts were a record £4,000 for the New Road ground.

WORCESTERSHIRE v AUSTRALIANS

Worcestershire

D.Kenyon	lbw b Lindwall	0	(2) st Tallon b McCool		17
E.Cooper	c Hassett b Toshack	51	(1) lbw b Toshack		22
C.H.Palmer	c Johnson b Toshack	85	st Tallon b McCool		34
R.E.S.Wyatt	st Tallon b McCool	18	absent ill		0
L.Outschoorn	b Lindwall	1	(4) c Tallon b Barnes		54
A.F.T.White*	c Tallon b Miller	1	c Barnes b McCool		11
R.O.Jenkins	b Johnson	7	lbw b Johnson		21
R.Howorth	not out	37	(5) lbw b McCool		0
R.T.D.Perks	c Toshack b McCool	0	(8) c Barnes b Johnson		27
H.Yarnold†	c Barnes b Johnson	15	(9) c Lindwall b Johnson		11
P.F.Jackson	c Barnes b Johnson	1	(10) not out		9
Extras	b 7, lb 10	17	b 4, lb 1, w 1		6
Total	(269 mins)	233	(228 mins)		212

Fall of wickets (1): 1-0, 2-137, 3-158, 4-159, 5-164, 6-178, 7-178, 8-178, 9-219, 10-233
Fall of wickets (2): 1-41, 2-41, 3-108, 4-108, 5-122, 6-165, 7-165, 8-195, 9-212

Australians

S.G.Barnes	lbw b Howorth	44
A.R.Morris	c Jenkins b Jackson	138
D.G.Bradman*	b Jackson	107
R.R.Lindwall	lbw b Jackson	32
C.L.McCool	b Jackson	0
D.Tallon†	b Jackson	4
A.L.Hassett	c Wyatt b Jackson	35
W.A.Brown	st Yarnold b Howorth	25
K.R.Miller	not out	50
I.W.Johnson	not out	12
E.R.H.Toshack	did not bat	
Extras	b 6, lb 5, w 4	15
Total	(398 mins) 8 wkts dec.	462

Fall of wickets: 1-79, 2-265, 3-297, 4-314, 5-320, 6-335, 7-388, 8-402

Australians Bowling

	O	M	R	W	O	M	R	W	
Lindwall	15	2	41	2	3	0	19	0	
Miller	12	1	36	1	8	3	18	0	
McCool	19	9	38	2	17	5	29	4	(1w)
Toshack	14	3	39	2	18	8	40	1	
Johnson	23	8	52	3	13.3	1	75	3	
Barnes	9	6	10	0	8	2	25	1	

Worcestershire Bowling

	O	M	R	W	
Perks	26	3	95	0	(4w)
Palmer	16	5	56	0	
Wyatt	1	0	4	0	
Howorth	38	6	109	2	
Jackson	39	4	135	6	
Jenkins	7	0	47	0	
Outschoorn	1	0	1	0	

Umpires: C.F.Root and D.Davies
Close of play: 1st day: Australians (1) 10-0 (Barnes 6, Morris 4); 2nd day: Australians (2) 377-6 (Hassett 33, Brown 12)

E.Cooper and C.H.Palmer added 137 in 132 minutes for the 2nd wicket in the first innings. A.R.Morris scored 138 in 275 minutes with 19 fours. D.G.Bradman scored 107 in 152 minutes with 15 fours. A.R.Morris and D.G.Bradman added 186 in 152 minutes for the 2nd wicket.

LEICESTERSHIRE v AUSTRALIANS

Played at Grace Road, Leicester on May 1, 3, 4 1948
Australians won by an innings and 171 runs
Toss won by Australians

The cold weather continued when the tourists went to Grace Road. On the Saturday, they hit 407 for eight, with Miller not out 175. Bradman looked certain to make another hundred, but was caught behind at 81, scored at nearly one a minute. Miller started well; after Bradman was out and the rest of the batting floundered against their fellow Australians, Jackson and Walsh, Miller played very responsibly.

On the second morning he returned to the attack to make certain of a double hundred before the innings ended. Ring's leg-breaks and the off-spin of Johnson were altogether too much for the county batsmen. Leicestershire had to rely on a few lusty blows from Walsh to reach three figures in the first innings. The follow on was enforced and five second innings wickets had gone down before Monday's close.

Rain prevented any play until 2.30 on the third day; it then took the tourists just an hour to finish off the innings. Johnson bowled to a leg trap which seemed to worry the batsmen unduly, with the exception of Jackson who carried out his bat. This was to prove the only major match in which Bradman did not go in first wicket down. On the first day a record crowd of 16,000 watched the game - the 1938 fixture had, of course, been played at Aylestone Road.

LEICESTERSHIRE v AUSTRALIANS

Australians

S.G.Barnes	lbw b Sperry	78
W.A.Brown	b Jackson	26
K.R.Miller	not out	202
D.G.Bradman*	c Corrall b Etherington	81
R.N.Harvey	lbw b Walsh	12
R.A.Hamence	st Corrall b Walsh	7
S.J.E.Loxton	lbw b Jackson	4
I.W.Johnson	c Lester b Jackson	6
R.A.Saggers†	c Lester b Jackson	6
D.T.Ring	run out	2
W.A.Johnston	st Corrall b Jackson	12
Extras	b 10, nb 2	12
Total	(372 mins)	448

Fall of wickets: 1-46, 2-157, 3-316, 4-344, 5-366, 6-373, 7-397, 8-407, 9-411, 10-448

Leicestershire

L.G.Berry*	b Loxton	1	c Miller b Johnson		20
G.Lester	c Saggers b Ring	19	c Ring b Johnson		40
F.T.Prentice	c Barnes b Johnson	22	c and b Johnson		3
M.Tompkin	lbw b Ring	15	c Johnston b Johnson		5
V.E.Jackson	c Brown b Johnson	17	not out		31
W.B.Cornock	run out	10	b Johnson		6
T.A.Chapman	c Loxton b Ring	4	c Saggers b Johnson		16
J.E.Walsh	c Loxton b Ring	33	lbw b Johnston		1
M.W.Etherington	not out	0	b Johnson		0
P.Corrall†	run out	0	c Bradman b Miller		8
J.Sperry	c Barnes b Ring	0	b Miller		13
Extras	b 4, lb 5	9	b 2, lb 1, w 1		4
Total	(155 mins)	130	(205 mins)		147

Fall of wickets (1): 1-1, 2-34, 3-56, 4-74, 5-79, 6-90, 7-130, 8-130, 9-130, 10-130
Fall of wickets (2): 1-45, 2-66, 3-66, 4-77, 5-83, 6-113, 7-116, 8-117, 9-131, 10-147

Leicestershire Bowling

	O	M	R	W	
Sperry	27	5	84	1	(1nb)
Etherington	26	2	94	1	
Cornock	3	0	13	0	
Jackson	37.2	3	91	5	
Walsh	29	0	125	2	
Lester	7	0	29	0	(1nb)

Australians Bowling

	O	M	R	W	O	M	R	"	
Johnston	6	0	15	0	27	10	42	1	
Loxton	6	1	11	1	7	3	12	0	
Johnson	23	9	50	2	21	8	42	7	
Ring	22.5	9	45	5	11	2	26	0	(1w)
Barnes					4	0	11	0	
Miller					4.1	1	10	2	

Umpires: A.Skelding and C.N.Woolley
Close of Play: 1st day: Australians 407-8 (Miller 175, Ring 0); 2nd day: Leicestershire (2) 113-5 (Jackson 19, Chapman 16)

K.R.Miller scored 202 in 325 minutes with 1 six and 16 fours. K.R.Miller and D.G.Bradman added 159 in 112 minutes for the 3rd wicket.

YORKSHIRE v AUSTRALIANS

Played at Bradford on May 5, 6 1948
Australians won by 4 wickets
Toss won by Yorkshire

The weather conditions remained most unpleasant for the third game of the tour; this time the wicket was also very lively. The pitch was uncovered and therefore, due to previous rain, play could not begin until 2.30 on the first day. Sellars won the toss and chose to bat. If anything it was colder than at either Worcester or Leicester. The ball soon became so greasy that Miller bowled off-breaks; Loxton slipped trying to achieve some pace and strained a groin muscle after a single over. Hutton found batting conditions very trying. He scored a single, then went an hour before making a second run. The left-handed Watson looked promising for a short while though by tea the total was 38 for three. The Australians fared even worse and were 38 for four at the close.

Miller hit out bravely on the second morning, then the off-spin of Smailes aided by Wardle finished the innings. Johnston was virtually unplayable as the wicket dried out during the county's second innings, the Australians therefore required just 60 for victory. Six wickets fell for 31 and defeat was ominously close. It was worth noting that Wardle rubbed the new ball in the dirt before opening the Yorkshire attack with Smailes. Fatally for the home side, Hutton dropped Harvey at short leg when the youngster had made a single. Hutton fell forward and clutched the ball but it bounced out of his grasp. Harvey swept the next ball for four and with the help of Tallon took his side to victory. It had been pointed out that Loxton would not bat, so effectively only three wickets remained. Attendance on the first day was 6,500.

YORKSHIRE v AUSTRALIANS

Yorkshire

L.Hutton	c Harvey b Miller	5	c Hamence b Johnston	11
H.Halliday	b Johnston	15	c Brown b Miller	1
E.I.Lester	c Brown b Miller	0	hit wkt b Johnston	16
W.Watson	b Johnston	6	(5) b Johnston	1
A.Coxon	b Johnston	14	(6) lbw b Johnston	9
T.F.Smailes	c Brown b Miller	3	(7) b Miller	6
R.Aspinall	c Harvey b Johnston	13	(4) b Miller	10
A.B.Sellars*	c Brown b Miller	0	b Lindwall	21
J.H.Wardle	b Miller	0	b Johnston	0
D.V.Brennan†	not out	6	not out	3
E.P.Robinson	c Lindwall b Miller	7	b Johnston	0
Extras	lb 1, nb 1	2	b 11	11
Total	(159 mins)	71	(108 mins)	89

Fall of wickets (1): 1-21, 2-22, 3-22, 4-40, 5-45, 6-49, 7-50, 8-50, 9-58, 10-71
Fall of wickets (2): 1-16, 2-17, 3-42, 4-42, 5-47, 6-62, 7-66, 8-72, 9-88, 10-89

Australians

W.A.Brown	lbw b Smailes	13	(2) lbw b Smailes	2
A.R.Morris	c and b Smailes	17	(1) c Hutton b Smailes	3
A.L.Hassett*	b Smailes	0	(4) c Sellars b Smailes	12
R.A.Hamence	c Aspinall b Smailes	12	(5) run out	1
R.N.Harvey	c Sellars b Robinson	7	(6) not out	18
K.R.Miller	c Watson b Smailes	34	(3) c Halliday b Wardle	2
C.L.McCool	st Brennan b Wardle	3	c and b Wardle	5
R.R.Lindwall	b Smailes	0		
D.Tallon†	c Robinson b Wardle	10	(8) not out	17
W.A.Johnston	not out	5		
S.J.E.Loxton	absent injured	0		
Extras			b 3	3
Total	(95 mins)	101	(65 mins) 6 wkts	63

Fall of wickets (1): 1-24, 2-24, 3-31, 4-38, 5-74, 6-78, 7-86, 8-86, 9-101
Fall of wickets (2): 1-4, 2-5, 3-13, 4-20, 5-20, 6-31

Australians Bowling

	O	M	R	W		O	M	R	W
Johnston	26	14	22	4		15.2	7	18	6
Miller	23.3	7	42	6		16	3	49	3
Loxton	1	1	0	0	(1nb)				
Lindwall	4	1	5	0		5	1	11	1

Yorkshire Bowling

	O	M	R	W	O	M	R	W
Aspinall	2	0	5	0				
Coxon	2	0	3	0				
Smailes	14	2	51	6	11.5	2	32	3
Wardle	8.1	2	28	2	12	1	28	2
Robinson	5	1	14	1				

Umpires: H.Elliott and E.Cooke.
Close of Play: Australians (1) 38-4 (Hamence 1)

SURREY v AUSTRALIANS

Played at The Oval on May 8, 10, 11 1948
Australians won by an innings and 296 runs
Toss won by Australians

The wicket at The Oval was in complete contrast to Park Avenue, a batsmen's paradise. Bradman returned to the team, won the toss and batted. By the time stumps were drawn the total was 479 for four. Cutting and hooking with nonchalant ease, Barnes hit eighteen fours in his stay of four and a quarter hours. Morris helped him with an opening partnership of 136, then Bradman arrived. Surridge attempted bouncers; Bradman swatted them away in disgust. McMahon, left-arm spinner, another Australian in county cricket, occasionally beat the bat, but in between was ruthlessly dispatched to the boundary. Bradman's innings lasted two and three-quarter hours and he hit fifteen fours. Bedser eventually clean bowled him playing back.

Hassett completed a hundred on the second day. Bedser earned three more wickets. Lindwall quickly dismissed Fletcher and Squires when Surrey began batting; the wicket was now dry and dusty giving the bowlers some assistance. Fishlock, who was totally ignored by the English selectors, played a very sound knock. Johnson and Ring dealt with the rest of the pack. Following on Surrey were 25 for two by the close; in addition Barling, attempting a hook to a ball from Johnston, had deflected the ball onto his forehead and retired when the score was 21 for two.

The only batting worth recalling during the last day came from Squires. He was eventually removed by the acrobatics of Harvey, who repeated the trick when catching Surridge.

During the second day came the incident which has gone down in cricketing legend. A stray dog interrupted play. It was rounded up by Barnes and carried to umpire Skelding, whose aversion to dogs is celebrated: Skelding had umpired at Leicester and Barnes, dismayed by Skelding's lbw decision, had told him he required a dog. Now one miraculously appeared!

SURREY v AUSTRALIANS

Australians

S.G.Barnes	lbw b Squires	176
A.R.Morris	lbw b McMahon	65
D.G.Bradman*	b Bedser	146
A.L.Hassett	b Bedser	110
R.N.Harvey	b McMahon	7
I.W.Johnson	c Fishlock b Bedser	46
R.R.Lindwall	b Bedser	4
D.Tallon†	not out	50
D.T.Ring	b McMahon	2
W.A.Johnston	lbw b Laker	6
E.R.H.Toshack	c and b McMahon	8
Extras	b 6, lb 5, nb 1	12

Total	(472 mins)	632

Fall of wickets: 1-136, 2-343, 3-403, 4-414, 5-543, 6-553, 7-568, 8-582, 9-599, 10-632

Surrey

L.B.Fishlock	not out	81	c Tallon b Johnston	5
D.G.W.Fletcher	b Lindwall	1	b Johnston	2
H.S.Squires	lbw b Lindwall	3	c Harvey b Johnson	54
T.H.Barling	c Ring b Johnson	10	retired hurt	10
M.R.Barton	c Barnes b Johnson	4	c Johnston b Lindwall	15
A.J.W.McIntyre†	c and b Ring	6	c Tallon b Toshack	23
E.R.T.Holmes*	b Johnson	0	b Johnson	3
J.C.Laker	b Ring	9	c Johnson b Johnston	20
A.V.Bedser	c Morris b Ring	2	c Johnson b Johnston	20
W.S.Surridge	c Harvey b Johnson	15	c Harvey b Johnson	20
J.W.McMahon	lbw b Johnson	0	not out	0
Extras	b 9, lb 1	10	b 15, lb 6, w 1, nb 1	23
		----		----
Total	(170 mins)	141	(222 mins)	195

Fall of wickets (1): 1-7, 2-15, 3-40, 4-52, 5-65, 6-66, 7-95, 8-103, 9-124, 10-141
Fall of wickets (2): 1-4, 2-11, 3-62, 4-129, 5-132, 6-132, 7-172, 8-187, 9-195

Surrey Bowling

	O	M	R	W	
Bedser	40	9	104	4	(1nb)
Surridge	26	4	86	0	
Laker	37	4	137	1	
Squires	10	0	62	1	
McMahon	42.2	1	210	4	
Holmes	4	0	21	0	

Australians Bowling

	O	M	R	W	O	M	R	W	
Lindwall	8	3	10	2	17	3	35	1	(1nb)
Johnston	7	2	15	0	22	9	40	4	
Toshack	10	4	19	0	15	3	35	1	
Johnson	18.2	2	53	5	9.5	2	40	3	(1w)
Ring	14	4	34	3	5	1	22	0	

Umpires: H.Baldwin and A.Skelding
Close of Play: 1st day: Australians (1) 479-4 (Hassett 61, Johnson 19); 2nd day: Surrey (2) 25-2 (Squires 3, Barton 1)

S.G.Barnes scored 176 in 256 minutes with 18 fours. D.G.Bradman scored 146 in 174 minutes with 15 fours. A.L.Hassett scored 110 in 173 minutes with 5 fours. S.G.Barnes and A.R.Morris added 136 in 116 minutes for the 1st wicket. S.G.Barnes and D.G.Bradman added 207 in 138 minutes for the 2nd wicket. A.L.Hassett and I.W.Johnson added 129 in 102 minutes for the 5th wicket.

CAMBRIDGE UNIVERSITY v AUSTRALIANS

Played at Fenner's, Cambridge on May 12, 13, 14 1948
Australians won by an innings and 51 runs
Toss won by Cambridge University

Glorious weather and a perfect pitch greeted the tourists at Fenner's. The students batted first. Doggart played some good strokes against Lindwall and later Insole scored well on the leg-side; before tea however the Australians had started their innings. Morris was brilliantly caught by Pearsall at short leg. It was the only wicket to fall for the rest of the day.

Brown quietly added to his score and reached exactly 200 in nearly five hours including sixteen fours. Hamence hit hard for his 92 and Hassett was going along nicely when the innings was closed. Seven wickets fell in the Cambridge second innings before stumps, Dewes made a competent 40 and Bailey was undefeated. Owing to a strained muscle sustained whilst fielding, Lindwall only bowled a single over and the spinners McCool and Ring operated for much of the time. Bailey batted in all about two and a half hours and hit nine fours, the game however finished about an hour before lunch on the third morning. Again record crowds came to watch the tourists, nearly 25,000 coming on the three days.

CAMBRIDGE UNIVERSITY v AUSTRALIANS

Cambridge University

J.Pepper	c Miller b Tochack	28	st Saggers b McCool	16
J.G.Dewes	b Miller	6	c and b McCool	40
G.H.G.Doggart	c Hassett b Toshack	33	st Saggers b McCool	6
G.M.Shuttleworth	c Saggers b Ring	7	b McCool	4
T.E.Bailey	run out	16	not out	66
B.C.Elgood	b Miller	12	b Miller	13
D.J.Insole†	c Miller b Lindwall	33	b McCool	9
J.M.Mills*	c Hamence b Miller	13	c sub (Johnston) b McCool	15
B.J.K.Pryor	not out	9	run out	13
W.H.Griffiths	b Miller	1	lbw b Miller	0
R.D.Pearsall	b Miller	0	c Miller b McCool	6
Extras	lb 6, nb 3	9	b 6, lb 2	8
Total	(209 mins)	167	(249 mins)	196

Fall of wickets (1): 1-12, 2-61, 3-76, 4-76, 5-96, 6-129, 7-150, 8-159, 9-167, 10-167
Fall of wickets (2): 1-36, 2-56, 3-60, 4-73, 5-99, 6-113, 7-141, 8-176, 9-184, 10-196

Australians

W.A.Brown	c Pearsall b Griffiths	200
A.R.Morris	c Pearsall b Mills	26
R.A.Hamence	c Insole b Griffiths	92
R.N.Harvey	run out	16
A.L.Hassett*	not out	61
K.R.Miller	did not bat	
C.L.McCool	did not bat	
R.R.Lindwall	did not bat	
R.A.Saggers†	did not bat	
D.T.Ring	did not bat	
E.R.H.Toshack	did not bat	
Extras	b 12, lb 1, w 1, nb 5	19
Total	(294 mins) 4 wkts dec.	414

Fall of wickets: 1-64, 2-240, 3-274, 4-414

Australians Bowling

	O	M	R	W		O	M	R	W
Lindwall	8	1	31	1	(1nb)	1	0	2	0
Miller	21.2	4	46	5		13	3	29	2
Toshack	17	7	32	2	(1nb)	8	4	9	0
McCool	15	5	31	0		33.5	9	78	7
Ring	11	4	18	1	(1nb)	33	12	52	0
Morris						5	2	11	0
Hamence						3	0	7	0

Cambridge University Bowling

	O	M	R	W	
Bailey	15	1	43	0	(5nb)
Griffiths	32	4	138	2	
Pearsall	13	1	50	0	
Mills	25	4	88	1	
Pryor	13	0	59	0	(1w)
Doggart	6	1	17	0	

Umpires: F.S.Lee and H.Palmer
Close of play: 1st day Australians 184-1 (Brown 87, Hamence 60): 2nd day: Cambridge University (2) 144-7 (Bailey 34, Pryor 1)

R.D.Pearsall was out 1st ball in the first innings. W.A.Brown scored 200 in 294 minutes with 16 fours.
W.A.Brown and R.A.Hamence added 176 in 148 minutes for the 2nd wicket. W.A.Brown and A.L.Hasset added 140 in 89 minutes for the 4th wicket.

ESSEX v AUSTRALIANS

Played at Southend on May 15, 17 1948
Australians won by an innings and 451 runs
Toss won by Australians

The Australians went to Southend for the Whitsun holiday and broke all records. In a day's play lasting 350 minutes they scored 721. The breakdown of that total reads:

100 in 74	minutes	500 in 247	minutes
200 in 118		600 in 286	
300 in 170		650 in 297	
351 in 189		700 in 338	
451 in 220		721 in 350	

Another way of looking at it is:

Lunch	202-1	Brown 77, Bradman 42
Tea	493-4	Hamence 44, Loxton 26
Close	721	

Barnes and Brown began with an opening partnership of 145 in 97 minutes; Bradman and Brown hit 219 in 84 minutes and later Loxton and Saggers reached 166 in 66 minutes for the 6th wicket. Bradman was in total command, his 187 coming in 124 minutes with 32 fours and a five. Brown batted 192 minutes with 15 fours. Miller was clearly under the impression that the game was something of a farce and took guard in a very offhand manner, then seemed to intentionally miss the first ball he received and was bowled. Bailey, who had played for Cambridge in the previous game, was a last minute selection for Essex. His bowling gave no trouble and a finger injury whilst fielding meant that he was unable to bat.

On the Bank Holiday Monday someone raised the Essex flag upside down. It was a clear signal to their batsmen who failed utterly on a still easy wicket. The Essex captain, Pearce, batted well in the second innings and Peter Smith hit out bravely but the game didn't go into a third day. Still the receipts and attendance figures were records: £3,482 and 32,000.

ESSEX v AUSTRALIANS

Australians

S.G.Barnes	hit wkt b R.Smith	79
W.A.Brown	c Horsfall b Bailey	153
D.G.Bradman*	b T.P.B.Smith	187
K.R.Miller	b Bailey	0
R.A.Hamence	c T.P.B.Smith b R.Smith	46
S.J.E.Loxton	c Rist b Vigar	120
R.A.Saggers†	not out	104
I.W.Johnson	st Rist b T.P.B.Smith	9
D.T.Ring	c Vigar b T.P.B.Smith	1
W.A.Johnston	b Vigar	9
E.R.H.Toshack	c Vigar b T.P.B.Smith	4
Extras	b 7, nb 2	9
Total	(350 mins)	721

Fall of wickets: 1-145, 2-364, 3-364, 4-452, 5-498, 6-664, 7-686, 8-692, 9-716, 10-721

Essex

T.C.Dodds	c Ring b Miller	0	b Toshack	16
S.J.Cray	b Miller	5	b Johnson	15
A.V.Avery	b Johnston	10	c Brown b Johnson	3
F.H.Vigar	c Saggers b Miller	0	c Johnson b Toshack	0
R.Horsfall	b Toshack	11	b Johnson	8
T.N.Pearce*	c Miller b Toshack	8	c and b Johnson	71
R.Smith	c Barnes b Toshack	25	c Ring b Johnson	0
T.P.B.Smith	b Toshack	3	lbw b Barnes	54
F.H.Rist†	c Barnes b Toshack	8	b Johnson	1
E.Price	not out	4	not out	4
T.E.Bailey	absent injured	0	absent injured	0
Extras	b 2, lb 6, nb 1	9	b 6, lb 3, nb 6	15
Total	(108 mins)	83	(202 mins)	187

Fall of wickets (1): 1-0, 2-13, 3-13, 4-19, 5-30, 6-47, 7-63, 8-74, 9-83
Fall of wickets (2): 1-24, 2-32, 3-35, 4-36, 5-46, 6-46, 7-177, 8-183, 9-187

Essex Bowling

	O	M	R	W	
Bailey	21	1	129	2	
R.Smith	37	2	169	2	(2nb)
T.P.B.Smith	38	0	192	4	
Price	20	0	156	0	
Vigar	13	1	66	2	

Australians Bowling

	O	M	R	W		O	M	R	W	
Miller	8	3	14	3		2	1	4	0	
Johnston	7	1	10	1		10	4	26	0	
Ring	11	4	19	0	(1nb)	7	3	16	0	(1nb)
Toshack	10.5	0	31	5		17	2	50	2	(3nb)
Loxton						12	3	28	0	(2nb)
Johnson						21	6	37	6	
Barnes						9.4	5	11	1	

Umpires: W.H.Ashdown and D.Hendren
Close of play: 1st day: Australians all out

W.A.Brown scored 153 in 192 minutes with 15 fours. D.G.Bradman scored 187 in 124 minutes with 1 five and 32 fours. S.J.E.Loxton scored 120 in 88 minutes with 1 six and 14 fours. R.A.Saggers scored 104 in 104 minutes with 8 fours. S.G.Barnes and W.A.Brown added 145 in 97 minutes for the 1st wicket. W.A.Brown and D.G.Bradman added 219 in 84 minutes for the 2nd wicket. S.J.E.Loxton and R.A.Saggers added 166 in 66 minutes for the 6th wicket. T.N.Pearce and T.P.B.Smith added 131 in 98 minutes for the 7th wicket in the second innings. F.H.Vigar was out 1st ball in the first innings and 2nd ball in the second innings.

OXFORD UNIVERSITY v AUSTRALIANS

Played at Christ Church Ground, Oxford on May 19, 20, 21 1948
Australians won by an innings and 90 runs
Toss won by Australians

In order to take a 'gate', the match was played on the Christ Church ground. There were four Dominion cricketers in the University side: Travers, van Ryneveld, Kardar and Robinson. Kardar had played Test cricket for India. Hassett won the toss and batted first on a warm, sunny day. Brown and Morris began with a stand of 139, but after that the run flood failed to materialise. Kardar bowled some accurate left-arm deliveries round the wicket and the very tall Whitcombe bowled impressively in the style of Farnes. The first five wickets were gone for 214, but, unfortunately for the students, two dropped catches allowed later batsmen to retrieve the situation. Loxton and McCool added 91 for the 6th wicket and Loxton and Ring put on a further 87 for the 8th.

When the home side batted, the wicket became increasingly helpful to the spinners. Keighley, and Kardar in both innings, were the only Oxford men to master the bowling for any length of time. The match was won by an innings. Hassett played a joke on the University captain, requesting a spiked roller - Pawson went off to see if one was available!

OXFORD UNIVERSITY v AUSTRALIANS

Australians

W.A.Brown	lbw b Kardar	108
A.R.Morris	run out	64
R.N.Harvey	c Pawson b Kardar	23
A.L.Hassett*	c Robinson b Whitcombe	0
R.A.Hamence	c Davidson b Mallett	3
S.J.E.Loxton	not out	79
C.L.McCool	b Whitcombe	50
R.A.Saggers†	b Travers	6
D.T.Ring	b Travers	53
E.R.H.Toshack	c and b Mallett	2
W.A.Johnston	b Mallett	13
Extras	b 25, lb 4, nb 1	30
Total	(377 mins)	431

Fall of wickets: 1-139, 2-173, 3-173, 4-206, 5-214, 6-305, 7-317, 8-404, 9-413, 10-431

Oxford University

W.G.Keighley	c Loxton b Ring	36	lbw b McCool	9
N.C.F.Bloy	c Harvey b Loxton	7	b Johnston	13
H.E.Webb	c Saggers b Johnston	1	c Brown b Johnston	3
H.A.Pawson*	b Johnston	0	c McCool b Toshack	15
A.H.Kardar	c Hamence b McCool	54	b Morris	29
C.B.Van Ryneveld	run out	32	lbw b Toshack	14
B.H.Travers	c McCool b Toshack	6	b Toshack	0
P.A.Whitcombe	run out	26	lbw b Loxton	26
A.W.H.Mallett	b Toshack	0	c Hassett b McCool	20
H.B.Robinson	c Hassett b Toshack	3	not out	13
W.W.Davidson†	not out	1	b McCool	2
Extras	b 6, lb 8, nb 5	19	b 8, lb 2, w 2	12
Total	(215 mins)	185	(189 mins)	156

Fall of wickets (1): 1-16, 2-19, 3-19, 4-94, 5-129, 6-146, 7-151, 8-155, 9-180, 10-185
Fall of wickets (2): 1-19, 2-23, 3-33, 4-53, 5-75, 6-75, 7-118, 8-124, 9-153, 10-156

Oxford University Bowling

	O	M	R	W	
Whitcombe	23	3	83	2	
Mallett	45	10	110	3	
Travers	11	3	36	2	
Kardar	46	11	118	2	
Robinson	11	1	54	0	(1nb)

Australians Bowling

	O	M	R	W		O	M	R	W	
Johnston	21	6	40	2		21	7	44	2	(1w)
Loxton	5	1	14	1		8	1	16	1	
Ring	18	4	39	1		5	0	12	0	(1w)
Toshack	22	4	34	3	(5nb)	16	6	37	3	
McCool	9	1	39	1		12.1	3	29	3	
Morris						3	2	6	1	

Umpires: D.Hendren and C.V.Tarbox
Close of play: 1st day: Australians 404-8 (Loxton 70); 2nd day: Oxford University (2) 54-4 (Kardar 10, Van Ryneveld 1)

W.A.Brown scored 108 in 215 minutes with 11 fours. W.A.Brown and A.R.Morris added 139 in 112 minutes for the 1st wicket. B.H.Travers was out 1st ball in the second innings.

M.C.C. v AUSTRALIANS

Played at Lord's on May 22, 24, 25 1948
Australians won by an innings and 158 runs
Toss won by Australians

Over 30,000 attended on the first day, the gates being shut when the ground was full. The tourists took first use of an easy wicket. For some reason the pitch had been prepared right over to one side of the square, making a short boundary and the Australians took full advantage. Six hours cricket produced 407 runs for five wickets. Bradman and Barnes added 160 for the second wicket. Barnes took advantage of short deliveries on or about the leg stump, using his hook to great advantage. Bradman began rather shakily, but soon settled and was rather surprised to find himself caught on 98. The ball deflected off the wicketkeeper's glove and went into Edrich's hands at slip. Hassett played a charming innings.

On Monday morning Miller, 114 not out over the weekend, hit Laker for two sixes; Johnson and Lindwall hit the same bowler for three sixes each and 145 came in 82 minutes, including ten sixes.

Miller quickly had both Robertson and Edrich caught behind when M.C.C. batted; Compton also fell to a brilliant catch by Tallon, so the only batsman to impress was Hutton. He was caught at short square leg off Toshack, who bowled chiefly on the leg stump. The Englishmen were clearly intimidated by Barnes who fielded very close at short leg, with more often than not a foot actually on the wicket. The follow on was enforced. Hutton again batted well, but the two players from whom runs were expected, Compton and Edrich, made little impact. The total attendance at the match was nearly 60,000.

M.C.C. v AUSTRALIANS

Australians

S.G.Barnes	c Edrich b Cranston	81
A.R.Morris	lbw b Edrich	5
D.G.Bradman*	c Edrich b Deighton	98
A.L.Hassett	lbw b Young	51
K.R.Miller	c Donnelly b Laker	163
W.A.Brown	c Cranston b Laker	26
I.W.Johnson	lbw b Laker	80
C.L.McCool	c Edrich b Young	0
D.Tallon†	b Young	11
R.R.Lindwall	not out	29
E.R.H.Toshack	c Compton b Young	2
Extras	b 4, lb 2	6

Total	(445 mins)	552

Fall of wickets: 1-11, 2-171, 3-200, 4-280, 5-343, 6-498, 7-498, 8-512, 9-532, 10-552

M.C.C.

L.Hutton	c Hassett b Toshack	52	lbw b Johnson	64
J.D.B.Robertson	c Tallon b Miller	6	c Barnes b Miller	0
W.J.Edrich	c Tallon b Miller	4	lbw b Toshack	25
D.C.S.Compton	c Tallon b Toshack	26	c Johnson b Lindwall	20
M.P.Donnelly	lbw b Toshack	5	st Tallon b Johnson	16
N.W.D.Yardley*	b Lindwall	17	c Bradman b McCool	24
K.Cranston	c Hassett b Toshack	21	b Johnson	12
S.C.Griffith†	b Toshack	7	not out	10
J.H.G.Deighton	c Barnes b Toshack	0	b McCool	5
J.C.Laker	not out	16	c Morris b McCool	4
J.A.Young	c Lindwall b Miller	12	st Tallon b McCool	11
Extras	b 16, lb 6, nb 1	23	b 10, lb 4	14
		----		----
Total	(186 mins)	189	(179 mins)	205

Fall of wickets (1): 1-11, 2-17, 3-91, 4-103, 5-104, 6-144, 7-148, 8-159, 9-166, 10-189
Fall of wickets (2): 1-0, 2-40, 3-93, 4-128, 5-133, 6-159, 7-177, 8-187, 9-191, 10-205

M.C.C. Bowling

	O	M	R	W
Edrich	23	1	110	1
Deighton	22	4	88	1
Cranston	26	6	69	1
Young	55.2	12	147	4
Laker	37	10	127	3
Compton	3	1	5	0

Australians Bowling

	O	M	R	W		O	M	R	W
Lindwall	13	4	44	1		10	2	24	1
Miller	10.4	2	28	3		10	0	37	1
Toshack	27	8	51	6	(1nb)	15	3	43	1
Johnson	12	2	43	0		14	3	37	3
Barnes						4	0	15	0
McCool						7.2	0	35	4

Umpires: F.Chester and D.Davies
Close of play: 1st day: Australians 407-5 (Miller 114, Johnson 26); 2nd day: M.C.C. (2) 27-1 (Hutton 12, Edrich 13)

K.R.Miller scored 163 in 251 minutes with 3 sixes and 20 fours. S.G.Barnes and D.G.Bradman added 160 in 131 minutes for the 2nd wicket. K.R.Miller and I.W.Johnson added 155 in 105 minutes for the 6th wicket.

LANCASHIRE v AUSTRALIANS

Played at Old Trafford, Manchester on May 26 (no play), 27, 28 1948
Match drawn
Toss won by Lancashire

Rain washed out the first day at Old Trafford, but the game, although clearly a draw almost from the start, remains famous for the success of the unknown spin bowler, Malcolm Hilton. This nineteen year old in his third game for Lancashire dismissed Bradman cheaply in both innings.

Cranston won the toss and put the Australians in on a rain affected pitch. He did not however take full advantage of the conditions. Loxton and Harvey were able to retrieve the situation and at least get the total over 200.

Johnston kept the Lancashire batsmen under control on the third day and the final afternoon was spent watching the Australians bat - Bradman seemed a little too keen to put Hilton in his place and this unusual impetuosity caused the great man's downfall.

LANCASHIRE v AUSTRALIANS

Australians

S.G.Barnes	c Cranston b Hilton	31	c Roberts b Cranston		31
A.R.Morris	c E.H.Edrich b Pollard	22	c G.A.Edrich b Pollard		5
D.G.Bradman*	b Hilton	11	st E.H.Edrich b Hilton		43
I.W.Johnson	lbw b Hilton	5			
S.J.E.Loxton	b Roberts	39	(4) run out		52
R.N.Harvey	b Roberts	36	(5) not out		76
R.A.Hamence	b Pollard	2	(6) not out		49
R.A.Saggers†	not out	22			
R.R.Lindwall	c Lawton b Hilton	0			
W.A.Johnston	b Pollard	24			
E.R.H.Toshack	b Roberts	4			
Extras	b 6, lb 2	8	b 1, lb 2		3
Total	(215 mins)	204	(187 mins) 4 wkts		259

Fall of wickets (1): 1-37, 2-58, 3-72, 4-75, 5-136, 6-145, 7-167, 8-170, 9-195, 10-204
Fall of wickets (2): 1-25, 2-51, 3-125, 4-137

Lancashire

C.Washbrook	lbw b Toshack	33
W.Place	c Lindwall b Toshack	24
G.A.Edrich	b Johnston	55
J.T.Ikin	lbw b Lindwall	7
K.Cranston*	b Lindwall	14
E.H.Edrich†	b Johnston	5
A.Wharton	c Johnston b Lindwall	24
R.Pollard	c Hamence b Johnston	4
W.B.Roberts	st Saggers b Johnston	1
W.Lawton	b Johnston	0
M.J.Hilton	not out	0
Extras	b 11, lb 4	15
Total	(265 mins)	182

Fall of wickets: 1-48, 2-57, 3-91, 4-129, 5-144, 6-151, 7-161, 8-172, 9-180, 10-182

Lancashire Bowling

	O	M	R	W	O	M	R	W
Pollard	20	8	37	3	12	2	48	1
Lawton	9	4	21	0	8	1	43	0
Hilton	19	4	81	4	13	0	54	1
Roberts	21.4	4	57	3	14	3	35	0
Cranston					9	1	40	1
Wharton					7	1	20	0
Ikin					4	0	16	0

Australians Bowling

	O	M	R	W
Lindwall	19.3	6	44	3
Johnston	29	14	49	5
Toshack	28	8	40	2
Johnson	8	2	16	0
Loxton	8	1	18	0

Umpires: H.Elliott and C.N.Woolley
Close of play: 1st day: (no play); 2nd day: Lancashire 108-3 (G.H.Edrich 32, Cranston 5)

R.N.Harvey and R.A.Hamence added an unbroken 122 in 89 minutes for the 5th wicket in the second innings.

NOTTINGHAMSHIRE v AUSTRALIANS

Played at Trent Bridge, Nottingham on May 29, 31, June 1 1948
Match drawn
Toss won by Nottinghamshire

Lindwall bowled in devastating form on the opening day of the match, starting by capturing Keeton's wicket with the fourth ball of the match. His length and direction were faultless and he made the ball leave the bat in such a way as to deceive all but Simpson and Hardstaff. These two, batting in a very similar style, put up the only resistance adding 98 for the third wicket.

The Australians began Monday at 77 for the loss of Morris. Brown and Bradman the not out batsmen continued until after lunch. Bradman was bowled by Woodhead shortly after the interval, but Brown batted, in all, three and three-quarter hours for his 122. Before the close on the second day, Keeton retired hurt, struck on the chest or stomach by a ball from Lindwall which lifted. Stumps were drawn when he was injured, and he did not return on the following morning.

On the last day Simpson and Hardstaff continued the batting form of their first innings, the latter going on to compete the first hundred of the summer against the tourists. Hardstaff's innings contained 13 fours and a six.

NOTTINGHAMSHIRE v AUSTRALIANS

Nottinghamshire

W.W.Keeton	c Tallon b Lindwall	0	retired hurt		7
F.H.Winrow	b Lindwall	3	c Bradman b Johnson		31
R.T.Simpson	b Miller	74	st Tallon b Ring		70
J.Hardstaff	c Tallon b Lindwall	48	c Loxton b Ring		107
F.W.Stocks	b Lindwall	0	c Brown b Miller		6
P.F.Harvey	st Tallon b Ring	0	st Tallon b Ring		41
W.A.Sime*	c Lindwall b Johnson	8	b Johnson		0
H.J.Butler	st Tallon b Ring	4	c Loxton b Ring		13
A.Jepson	b Lindwall	4	c Brown b Johnson		3
F.G.Woodhead	not out	10	not out		2
E.A.Meads†	c Hassett b Lindwall	1	not out		8
Extras	b 15, lb 9, w 1, nb 2	27	b 5, lb 5, nb 1		11
Total	(195 mins)	179	(326 mins) 8 wkts		299

Fall of wickets (1): 1-0, 2-13, 3-111, 4-111, 5-118, 6-135, 7-146, 8-159, 9-161, 10-179
Fall of wickets (2): 1-69, 2-133, 3-163, 4-262, 5-262, 6-281, 7-285, 8-289

Australians

W.A.Brown	lbw b Jepson	122
A.R.Morris	lbw b Jepson	16
D.G.Bradman*	b Woodhead	86
C.L.McCool	b Winrow	17
A.L.Hassett	b Woodhead	44
K.R.Miller	b Woodhead	51
S.J.E.Loxton	run out	16
D.Tallon†	b Winrow	27
R.R.Lindwall	c Meads b Jepson	8
I.W.Johnson	b Jepson	0
D.T.Ring	not out	9
Extras	b 2, lb 1, nb 1	4
Total	(391 mins)	400

Fall of wickets: 1-32, 2-197, 3-235, 4-245, 5-326, 6-355, 7-355, 8-376, 9-376, 10-400

Australians Bowling

	O	M	R	W		O	M	R	W	
Lindwall	15.1	7	14	6	(1w)	14	3	31	0	
Miller	15	1	50	1		8	1	17	1	
Johnson	11	5	26	1		35	15	78	3	
Loxton	6	2	12	0	(2nb)	6	2	9	0	
McCool	8	2	19	0		21	5	49	0	
Ring	11	1	31	2		43	15	104	4	(1nb)

Nottinghamshire Bowling

	O	M	R	W	
Butler	32	4	98	0	(1nb)
Jepson	43	7	109	4	
Woodhead	32	3	92	3	
Harvey	16	1	43	0	
Winrow	13.2	2	54	2	

Umpires: G.M.Lee and T.J.Bartley
Close of play: 1st day: Australians 77-1 (Brown 38, Bradman 22); 2nd day: Nottinghamshire (2) 16-0 (Winrow 8)

W.A.Brown scored 122 in 228 minutes with 13 fours. W.A.Brown and D.G.Bradman added 165 in 157 minutes for the 2nd wicket. J.Hardstaff scored 107 in 180 minutes with 1 six and 13 fours.

HAMPSHIRE v AUSTRALIANS

Played at Southampton on June 2, 3, 4 1948
Australians won by 8 wickets
Toss won by Australians

Put in to bat on a drying wicket, Hampshire struggled against the left-arm medium pace of Johnston, who bowled all but four overs from one end, taking six for 74. The Australians lost their opening pair before the close on the first day.

On the Thursday, the spinners Knott and Bailey troubled all the visiting batsmen. Miller made 39, but only because he hit Knott for three successive sixes. Hampshire gained a first innings lead of 78, but were unable to build a substantial target for the tourists on the last day.

The Australians began their final innings shortly before lunch on the last day and immediately lost Barnes to the third ball of the innings. Johnson was sent in as a 'lunchwatchman', but then developed into an attacking batsman, hitting 74 out of 105 for the second wicket with three sixes and seven fours. Victory was achieved with about three-quarters of an hour left.

HAMPSHIRE v AUSTRALIANS

Hampshire

J.Arnold	b Loxton	48	c Johnson b Johnston	42
N.H.Rogers	c Barnes b Johnston	19	c Hassett b Miller	4
G.W.Dawson	c Barnes b Johnson	11	st Saggers b Johnston	6
C.G.A.Paris	c Johnson b Johnston	1	b Miller	1
J.Bailey	lbw b Johnston	25	lbw b Johnston	0
E.D.R.Eagar*	lbw b Johnson	15	b Miller	0
G.Hill	c Miller b Johnston	33	c and b Miller	23
C.J.Andrews†	b Johnston	4	c and b Johnston	10
V.J.Ransom	b Ring	11	b Miller	0
O.W.Herman	b Johnston	1	b Johnston	0
C.J.Knott	not out	1	not out	1
Extras	b 16, lb 8, nb 2	26	b 4, lb 12	16
Total	(221 mins)	195	(130 mins)	103

Fall of wickets (1): 1-36, 2-65, 3-72, 4-116, 5-123, 6-148, 7-167, 8-189, 9-194, 10-195
Fall of wickets (2): 1-17, 2-26, 3-33, 4-36, 5-45, 6-77, 7-95, 8-100, 9-101, 10-103

Australians

S.G.Barnes	lbw b Bailey	20	lbw b Knott	0
W.A.Brown	c Ransom b Herman	0	not out	81
A.L.Hassett*	lbw b Knott	26	(4) not out	27
K.R.Miller	b Knott	39		
S.J.E.Loxton	lbw b Bailey	0		
R.A.Hamence	b Knott	5		
I.W.Johnson	b Bailey	2	(3) b Hill	74
R.N.Harvey	c Hill b Bailey	1		
R.A.Saggers†	c Arnold b Knott	17		
D.T.Ring	c Dawson b Knott	0		
W.A.Johnston	not out	2		
Extras	b 4, nb 1	5		
Total	(139 mins)	117	(132 mins) 2 wkts	182

Fall of wickets (1): 1-6, 2-38, 3-70, 4-71, 5-91, 6-96, 7-98, 8-98, 9-98, 10-117
Fall of wickets (2): 1-0, 2-105

Australians Bowling

	O	M	R	W		O	M	R	W
Miller	19	6	39	0		12.5	4	25	5
Johnston	38.4	14	74	6		21	7	43	5
Johnson	17	6	35	2		4	1	13	0
Barnes	1	1	0	0					
Ring	7	1	19	1	(1nb)				
Loxton	3	1	2	1	(1nb)	5	3	6	0

Hampshire Bowling

	O	M	R	W		O	M	R	W
Herman	8	2	18	1	(1nb)	6	0	22	0
Ransom	5	2	10	0					
Knott	16.2	2	57	5		19	3	55	1
Bailey	17	6	27	4		18.5	2	91	0
Hill						6	1	14	1

Umpires: D.Davies and E.Robinson
Close of play: 1st day: Australians (1) 54-2 (Hassett 18, Miller 11); 2nd day: Hampshire (2) 5-0 (Arnold 3, Rogers 0)

W.A.Brown and I.W.Johnson added 105 in 76 minutes for the 2nd wicket in the second innings.

SUSSEX v AUSTRALIANS

Played at Hove on June 5, 7 1948
Australians won by an innings and 325 runs
Toss won by Sussex

Lindwall continued the form he had shown at Nottingham, completely routing Sussex twice. In the first innings, he hit the off stump five times and not a single Sussex batsman put up more than token resistance. In contrast Brown and Morris opened with a stand of 153. Morris's 184 contained 26 fours. Bradman replaced Brown and after two early escapes - a catch and a stumping - completed a century in two hours, with 12 fours. Harvey's hundred came in an even quicker time and he hit 16 fours.

When Australia declared, Lindwall took two wickets in the first over - John Langridge off the third ball and C.Oakes off the sixth. Parks survived the initial onslaught and took easy runs off Johnson before succumbing to Ring. The tail put up little fight and Toshack ended with the odd figures of 17 overs for six runs.

SUSSEX v AUSTRALIANS

Sussex

John G.Langridge	c Saggers b Lindwall	5	c Saggers b Lindwall		0
H.W.Parks	lbw b Loxton	4	b Ring		61
C.Oakes	b Lindwall	22	b Lindwall		0
G.Cox	lbw b Loxton	6	c sub (McCool) b Hamence		16
James Langridge	c Johnson b Loxton	0	lbw b Lindwall		15
J.Y.Oakes	b Lindwall	15	b Lindwall		1
H.T.Bartlett*	b Lindwall	8	lbw b Ring		2
S.C.Griffith†	b Lindwall	7	b Lindwall		24
P.A.D.Carey	b Lindwall	5	c Saggers b Ring		0
A.E.James	run out	4	not out		3
J.H.Cornford	not out	3	st Saggers b Hamence		1
Extras	lb 6, nb 1	7	b 5, lb 9, w 1		15
Total		86	(168 mins)		138

Fall of wickets (1): 1-7, 2-15, 3-34, 4-34, 5-56, 6-59, 7-73, 8-78, 9-81, 10-86
Fall of wickets (2): 1-0, 2-2, 3-24, 4-79, 5-95, 6-98, 7-109, 8-109, 9-133, 10-138

Australians

W.A.Brown	lbw b C.Oakes	44
A.R.Morris	c and b James Langridge	184
D.G.Bradman*	b Cornford	109
R.R.Lindwall	c Griffith b Cornford	57
R.N.Harvey	not out	100
R.A.Hamence	lbw b C.Oakes	34
I.W.Johnson	did not bat	
R.A.Saggers†	did not bat	
S.J.E.Loxton	did not bat	
D.T.Ring	did not bat	
E.R.H.Toshack	did not bat	
Extras	b 10, lb 10, nb 1	21
Total	(378 mins) 5 wkts dec.	549

Fall of wickets: 1-153, 2-342, 3-360, 4-453, 5-549

Australians Bowling

	O	M	R	W		O	M	R	W	
Lindwall	19.4	2	34	6		15	5	25	5	
Loxton	10	5	13	3	(1nb)					
Ring	2	0	9	0		13	4	42	3	
Toshack	15	4	23	0		17	14	6	0	
Hamence						7.3	3	13	2	(1w)
Johnson						11	4	37	0	

Sussex Bowling

	O	M	R	W	
Carey	23	1	102	0	
Cornford	31	6	122	2	
James	26	6	90	0	
Cox	16	3	54	0	
C.Oakes	15	2	60	2	(1nb)
James Langridge	16	1	68	1	
J.Y.Oakes	3	0	32	0	

Umpires: B.Flint and J.J.Hills
Close of play: Australians 254-1 (Morris 152, Bradman 43)

A.R.Morris scored 184 in 243 minutes with 26 fours. D.G.Bradman scored 109 in 124 minutes with 12 fours.
R.N.Harvey scored 100 in 118 minutes with 16 fours. W.A.Brown and A.R.Morris added 153 for the 1st wicket.
A.R.Morris and D.G.Bradman added 189 in 114 minutes for the 2nd wicket. McCool was fielding for Loxton when
he caught Cox. P.A.D.Carey was out 1st ball in the second innings.

ENGLAND v AUSTRALIA (1st Test)

Played at Trent Bridge, Nottingham on June 10, 11, 12, 14, 15 1948
Australia won by 8 wickets
Toss won by England

There were no surprises in either of the sides chosen for the match. The young hopefuls, Simpson and Harvey, were chosen as 12th men; England left out Wright who was suffering from lumbago (Pope had also been called up as a possible late replacement, but was not used). Yardley won the toss and decided to bat on a miserable day, rain delaying the start until 12.05. It was not long however before rain interrupted play and only 20 minutes action took place prior to lunch, when England were 13 for the loss of Hutton. Directly after lunch Edrich was dropped in the slips, but Washbrook then decided to hook and was caught on the long leg boundary. Edrich survived 75 minutes for 18; the light became extremely poor and Hardstaff was caught in the slips without scoring; Compton was bowled by Miller and half the England side were out for 48. Barnett, Yardley and Evans did little, to that the tea score was 75 for eight. After tea, Laker attacked whilst Bedser defended and the two Surrey bowlers doubled the total. The light had improved, but Bedser and Laker deserve full credit for their efforts. Laker reached 50 in an hour and was the last man out. Johnston playing his first Test in England had the very impressive figures of 25-11-36-5; Lindwall, owing to a strain, did not field in the latter part of the innings.

The weather was somewhat improved on the second day. Neither Australian batsman seemed overtroubled by the bowling, but Evans dropped Morris off Bedser. Laker took his first Test wicket in England in his third over, when Morris mispulled a ball on to his wicket. At lunch Australia were 104 for one, with Bradman beginning to look in good form. Barnes had the misfortune to edge a ball on to Evans' boot and the wicketkeeper held the catch as it rebounded, Laker being the bowler. In Laker's next over, the off-spinner had Miller caught in the slips. His figures were three for 22 and Australia were rather unhappy at 121 for three. The new ball was taken by Bedser and Edrich and successfully combated by Bradman and Brown. Yardley brought himself on to bowl and trapped Brown leg before. From then until the close Bradman and Hassett built up Australia's lead and had added 108. It was not exciting stuff and the crowd occasionally slow handclapped.

The sun shone on the third day and the ground was full. Play had scarcely settled into a routine when Bradman was caught at short fine leg. Hassett however remained until 3.30. He batted with competence, but he made his runs slowly: there was no need for haste. He reached 100 in 305 minutes batting. The later batsmen all made sensible contributions. Lindwall was absent when Australia fielded a second time, Harvey acting as substitute. England had two and a half hours to bat out the day. Washbrook was out almost at once, trying to hook. Edrich looked uncomfortable. He was caught behind by a ball that didn't turn. Compton joined Hutton and the pair batted well adding 82 runs at about one a minute until the close. Australia missed Lindwall; Miller tried some bouncers and the crowd, remembering Larwood, roared 'Bodyline'.

Monday was very humid with threats of a storm when play started. About midday there was a sudden heavy shower, but play was only held up for fifteen minutes. Miller bowled Hutton for 74 well made runs. Hardstaff came in; the light was terrible. After a few minutes the umpires sent the players in. There was a thirty minute stoppage, then, with the light seeming just as poor, play resumed. The fourth wicket had added 93. Hardstaff was caught at square leg off Toshack. O'Reilly described the light at this time as the worst in which Test cricket had ever been played. Barnett found his way to the wicket, but soon perished in the gloom. Yardley batted an hour for 22. Evans batted out time. Meanwhile Compton played quite brilliantly. He reached 100 in 227 minutes with 12 fours. He was dropped twice, but at the close was 154. Fingleton describes it as one of the grandest days of Test cricket he had known.

The light was little better on the fifth morning. Rain drove the players in shortly before midday. There was thirty minutes delay. Compton eventually fell on his wicket trying to hit a Miller bouncer to leg. The Middlesex batsman had made 184, his highest Test score to date and easily his best Test innings. Evans reached a well-merited 50, but at 2.40 England were all out and Australia had three hours in which to score 98 runs. Barnes seemed to want to finish the game by tea, but Morris looked unhappy against Bedser. The left-hander was soon deceived by an inswinger and clean bowled. Bradman, as in the first innings, was caught at backward short leg off Bedser - it was his first duck in Tests against England. The match ended without further mishap at 4.20.

The poor batting by England on the first day had sealed their fate, though the splendid batting of Compton and the absence of Lindwall nearly made a draw of it.

The Chairman of Nottinghamshire made a public apology to the Australians concerning the barracking they received when bowling bouncers. The press felt that in general the barracking was justified and would have been similar in Australia given the same circumstances.

A.L.Hassett
He scored a solid century in the First Test
Overall on the tour, he was second only to
Bradman in the batting averages.

D.G.Bradman scored 138 in 288 minutes with 10 fours. A.L.Hassett scored 137 in 354 minutes with 1 six and 20 fours. D.G.Bradman and A.L.Hassett added 120 in 163 minutes for the 5th wicket in the first innings. A.L.Hassett and R.R.Lindwall added 107 in 109 minutes for the 8th wicket in the first innings. D.C.S.Compton scored 184 in 410 minutes with 19 fours. L.Hutton and D.C.S.Compton added 111 in 121 minutes for the 3rd wicket in the second innings.

ENGLAND v AUSTRALIA (1st Test)

England

L.Hutton	b Miller	3	b Miller		74
C.Washbrook	c Brown b Lindwall	6	c Tallon b Miller		1
W.J.Edrich	b Johnston	18	c Tallon b Johnson		13
D.C.S.Compton	b Miller	19	hit wkt b Miller		184
J.Hardstaff	c Miller b Johnston	0	c Hassett b Toshack		43
C.J.Barnett	b Johnston	8	c Miller b Johnston		6
N.W.D.Yardley*	lbw b Toshack	3	c and b Johnston		22
T.G.Evans†	c Morris b Johnston	12	c Tallon b Johnston		50
J.C.Laker	c Tallon b Miller	63	b Miller		4
A.V.Bedser	c Brown b Johnston	22	not out		3
J.A.Young	not out	1	b Johnston		9
Extras	b 5, lb 5	10	b 12, lb 17, nb 3		32
Total	(225 mins)	165	(499 mins)		441

Fall of wickets (1): 1-9, 2-15, 3-46, 4-46, 5-48, 6-60, 7-74, 8-74, 9-163, 10-165
Fall of wickets (2): 1-5, 2-39, 3-150, 4-243, 5-264, 6-321, 7-405, 8-413, 9-423, 10-441

Australia

S.G.Barnes	c Evans b Laker	62	not out		64
A.R.Morris	b Laker	31	b Bedser		9
D.G.Bradman*	c Hutton b Bedser	138	c Hutton b Bedser		0
K.R.Miller	c Edrich b Laker	0			
W.A.Brown	lbw b Yardley	17			
A.L.Hassett	b Bedser	137	(4) not out		21
I.W.Johnson	b Laker	21			
D.Tallon†	c and b Young	10			
R.R.Lindwall	c Evans b Yardley	42			
W.A.Johnston	not out	17			
E.R.H.Toshack	lbw b Bedser	19			
Extras	b 9, lb 4, w 1, nb 1	15	lb 2, w 1, nb 1		4
Total	(606 mins)	509	(92 mins) 2 wkts		98

Fall of wickets (1): 1-73, 2-121, 3-121, 4-185, 5-305, 6-338, 7-365, 8-472, 9-476, 10-509
Fall of wickets (2): 1-38, 2-48

Australia Bowling

	O	M	R	W	O	M	R	W	
Lindwall	13	5	30	1					
Miller	19	8	38	3	44	10	125	4	
Johnston	25	11	36	5	59	12	147	4	
Toshack	14	8	28	1	33	14	60	1	(3nb)
Johnson	5	1	19	0	42	15	66	1	
Morris	3	1	4	0					
Barnes					5	2	11	0	

England Bowling

	O	M	R	W		O	M	R	W	
Edrich	18	1	72	0	(1w)	4	0	20	0	(1w)
Bedser	44.2	12	113	3	(1nb)	14.3	4	46	2	(1nb)
Barnett	17	5	36	0						
Young	60	28	79	1		10	3	28	0	
Laker	55	14	138	4						
Compton	5	0	24	0						
Yardley	17	6	32	2						

Umpires: F.Chester and E.Cooke
Close of play: 1st day: Australia (1) 17-0 (Barnes 6, Morris 10); 2nd day: Australia (1) 293-4 (Bradman 130, Hassett 41); 3rd day: England (2) 121-2 (Hutton 63, Compton 36); 4th day: England (2) 345-6 (Compton 154, Evans 10)

NORTHAMPTONSHIRE v AUSTRALIANS

Played at Northampton on June 16, 17, 18 1948
Australians won by an innings and 64 runs
Toss won by Australians

The tourists fielded a side that included all those who had not appeared in the First Test, but despite this 'Second Eleven' and interruptions from rain, the game was won with consummate ease.

Brookes was out to the fifth ball of the match and the county collapsed to 61 for seven. At this point two of their overseas players, Divecha, who was studying at Oxford and making his county debut, and C.B.Clarke, the former West Indian bowler, managed to defy Johnston and Johnson. 54 runs were added. 119 was however a very inadequate total and with Hassett in fine form the Australians took the lead having lost only Barnes. Hassett batted two and a half hours, hitting 17 fours in his 127. Later McCool attacked the bowling, which, apart from the fast medium deliveries of Nutter, was not too frightening.

Only five minutes play was possible before lunch on the second day, but Northants had virtually lost the match by the close, and the game was all over before the lunch interval on the third.

NORTHAMPTONSHIRE v AUSTRALIANS

Northamptonshire

D.Brookes	c McCool b Johnston	0	lbw b Johnston	44
N.Oldfield	lbw b Johnson	11	c McCool b Johnston	24
W.Barron	c Hassett b Loxton	18	c Morris b Johnston	4
J.E.Timms	b Loxton	3	lbw b Johnston	14
A.E.Nutter	b Johnson	7	(7) b Ring	9
V.Broderick	c Hassett b Johnson	8	lbw b Ring	21
A.W.Childs-Clarke*	c Harvey b Ring	8	(8) c Hassett b Johnson	14
R.V.Divecha	c Harvey b McCool	33	(5) lbw b Hamence	15
C.B.Clarke	b Johnston	19	c Johnston b Ring	2
R.G.Garlick	c Hassett b Johnston	2	c Hassett b Ring	0
K.Fiddling†	not out	0	not out	3
Extras	b 7, lb 2, w 1	10	b 7, lb 8, w 3, nb 1	19
Total	(163 mins)	119	(222 mins)	169

Fall of wickets (1): 1-0, 2-29, 3-35, 4-39, 5-50, 6-59, 7-61, 8-115, 9-118, 10-119
Fall of wickets (2): 1-42, 2-46, 3-78, 4-106, 5-118, 6-142, 7-151, 8-153, 9-155, 10-169

Australians

S.G.Barnes	c Childs-Clarke b Nutter	11
A.R.Morris	b Clarke	60
A.L.Hassett*	b Nutter	127
R.A.Hamence	b Nutter	34
S.J.E.Loxton	b Nutter	17
R.N.Harvey	c Barron b Divecha	14
C.L.McCool	not out	50
I.W.Johnson	c Clarke b Nutter	4
R.A.Saggers†	c and b Broderick	1
D.T.Ring	not out	18
W.A.Johnston	did not bat	
Extras	b 9, lb 5, w 1, nb 1	16
Total	(268 mins) 8 wkts dec.	352

Fall of wickets: 1-17, 2-139, 3-243, 4-248, 5-267, 6-284, 7-312, 8-313

Australians Bowling

	O	M	R	W		O	M	R	W	
Johnston	9.1	1	24	3		27	11	49	4	(1nb,1w)
Loxton	15	3	22	2	(1w)	4	0	7	0	(2w)
Johnson	13	7	13	3		23.4	5	46	1	
Ring	15	4	31	1		19	8	31	4	
McCool	8	2	19	1		3	1	2	0	
Barnes						3	0	4	0	
Hamence						4	1	11	1	

Northamptonshire Bowling

	O	M	R	W	
Divecha	20	2	65	1	(1w)
Nutter	23	3	57	5	(1nb)
Clarke	17	2	72	1	
Broderick	16	2	69	1	
Garlick	17	1	73	0	

Umpires: T.J.Bartley and C.N.Woolley
Close of play: 1st day: Australians 260-4 (Loxton 6, Harvey 11); 2nd day: Northamptonshire (2) 100-3 (Brookes 42, Divecha 6)

A.L.Hassett scored 127 in 155 minutes with 17 fours. A.R.Morris and A.L.Hassett added 122 in 87 minutes for the 2nd wicket. A.L.Hasset and R.A.Hamence added 104 in 59 minutes for the 3rd wicket.

YORKSHIRE v AUSTRALIANS

Played at Bramall Lane, Sheffield on June 19, 21, 22 1948
Match drawn
Toss won by Australians

Prior to the Second Test, the Australians played a second game against Yorkshire. Lindwall was still being rested ready for the greater conflict and as both Miller and Toshack suffered strains and could not bowl in the second innings, the visitors were happy to settle for a draw. Batting first, the Australians lost Barnes to Aspinall with the third delivery of the match. Bradman, Harvey and Hamence all made runs, but Yorkshire threw away their chances of success by dropping seven catches in the first innings.

Hutton and Halliday gave the county a sound start, but the remainder struggled against some good bowling by Johnston and Toshack. Barnes failed a second time, then Bradman and Brown added 154 for the second wicket - Yorkshire dropped several more catches. Miller was out second ball.

Bradman declared with just 70 minutes playing time left and Yorkshire batted out time.

YORKSHIRE v AUSTRALIANS

Australians

S.G.Barnes	b Aspinall	0	b Smailes	6
W.A.Brown	lbw b Wardle	19	b Yardley	113
D.G.Bradman*	c Yardley b Wardle	54	c Hutton b Aspinall	86
K.R.Miller	c Brennan b Coxon	20	b Aspinall	0
R.N.Harvey	c and b Coxon	49	c Halliday b Yardley	56
R.A.Hamence	c Brennan b Coxon	48	not out	6
C.L.McCool	lbw b Coxon	4	not out	7
R.A.Saggers†	c Yardley b Wardle	22		
D.T.Ring	b Aspinall	3		
W.A.Johnston	not out	15		
E.R.H.Toshack	c Watson b Aspinall	4		
Extras	b 4, lb 3, nb 4	11	b 6, lb 1, nb 4	11
Total	(290 mins)	249	(272 mins) 5 wkts dec.	285

Fall of wickets (1): 1-0, 2-67, 3-89, 4-123, 5-164, 6-168, 7-202, 8-207, 9-244, 10-249
Fall of wickets (2): 1-17, 2-171, 3-171, 4-263, 5-272

Yorkshire

L.Hutton	c Brown b Toshack	39		
H.Halliday	lbw b Toshack	28	(1) b Hamence	10
W.Watson	c Saggers b Johnston	20	(2) st Saggers b McCool	29
N.W.D.Yardley*	b Toshack	10		
E.I.Lester	st Saggers b Toshack	31	(6) not out	5
A.Coxon	c McCool b Johnston	21	(4) not out	16
R.Aspinall	b Toshack	11		
T.F.Smailes	c Saggers b Toshack	9	(5) c Harvey b McCool	5
J.H.Wardle	c McCool b Toshack	15		
D.V.Brennan†	c Ring b Johnston	6	(3) b Ring	17
E.P.Robinson	not out	1		
Extras	b 8, lb 7	15	b 2, lb 1	3
Total	(245 mins)	206	(69 mins) 4 wkts	85

Fall of wickets (1): 1-56, 2-81, 3-107, 4-107, 5-149, 6-169, 7-171, 8-189, 9-200, 10-206
Fall of wickets (2): 1-17, 2-59, 3-65, 4-78

Yorkshire Bowling

	O	M	R	W		O	M	R	W	
Aspinall	28.3	7	82	3	(2nb)	12	1	53	2	(4nb)
Coxon	26	5	66	4	(2nb)	25	9	47	0	
Smailes	10	1	36	0		24	8	57	1	
Wardle	20	8	37	3		20	5	66	0	
Robinson	8	4	17	0		5	0	17	0	
Hutton						1	0	3	0	
Yardley						7	2	9	2	
Halliday						5	0	22	0	

Australians Bowling

	O	M	R	W	O	M	R	W
Miller	6	4	4	0				
Johnston	41.1	10	101	3	3	1	15	0
Toshack	40	12	81	7				
Hamence	3	2	5	0	4	0	12	1
McCool					11	2	33	2
Ring					9	1	22	1

Umpires: J.T.Bell and K.McCanlis
Close of play: 1st day Yorkshire (1) 17-0 (Hutton 5, Halliday 12): 2nd day: Australians (2) 132-1 (Brown 56, Bradman 66)

W.A.Brown scored 113 in 251 minutes with 11 fours. W.A.Brown and D.G.Bradman added 154 in 154 minutes for the 2nd wicket in the second innings.

ENGLAND v AUSTRALIA (2nd Test)

Played at Lord's on June 24, 25, 26, 28, 29 1948
Australia won by 409 runs
Toss won by Australia

The England selectors made three changes for the Lord's Test. Wright was pronounced fit and replaced Young; Coxon, the Yorkshire fast bowler, came in for Barnett and the Warwickshire batsman Dollery replaced Hardstaff, who was doubtful due to a poisoned toe. Emmett of Gloucestershire replaced Simpson as 12th man. Australia retained the successful Trent Bridge side, though Miller owing to injury was played purely as a batsman. Harvey remained as 12th man.

Despite the heavy atmosphere which would clearly assist the seam bowlers, Bradman decided to bat. Coxon had Barnes caught at short fine leg in his second over. Morris looked more confident than Bradman, who was lucky to escape when 13. At lunch the score was 82 for one, both batsmen well settled. Soon after the interval Bradman fell to the Hutton-Bedser combination yet again. Morris continued to score and reached 105 before he was caught in the gulley after 209 minutes batting. He hit a six and 14 fours. England then took command. Hassett was yorked by Yardley; Miller was leg before to a ball he ignored and Brown was also out leg before. The first day belonged to England: Australia were 258 for seven.

On Friday the home country let the match slip. The Australian tail-enders hit runs using the most unorthodox methods; in 66 minutes another 92 runs were added. Lindwall then rubbed salt into the wound by destroying the top England batsmen. Washbrook was caught behind; Edrich was bowled after 70 minutes which produced three runs; Hutton was dismissed by Johnson. Dollery was out of his class and lasted two balls. Lindwall now had three for 18. Yardley joined Compton and the pair fought through to tea: England 129 for four, Compton 51, Yardley 42. After tea both batsmen soon went. The follow-on was just saved and one wicket remained at stumps.

On the third morning Lindwall resorted to bowling bumpers against Bedser, which was frowned on by all. Australia began their second innings at 12.05. Both Barnes and Morris had some luck as Yardley changed the bowling with unexpected speed - six bowling changes in the first hour. At lunch the total was 73 without loss. Morris's was the first wicket to fall; he attempted a sweep and was bowled. Barnes eventually fell to a catch on the boundary after 277 minutes batting with 14 fours and 2 sixes. Yardley was the bowler; next delivery he removed Hassett and Miller had to make a very undignified stroke to prevent a hat-trick. It was Bradman however who went next. He had made 89 when Bedser, for the fourth successive time, dismissed him, caught in the slips by Edrich.

The ground was again full when Australia resumed their innings on Monday morning. The grass was wet and the clouds threatening. After ten minutes play the cricketers retreated to the pavilion. It was an in and out day, but Australia hit 117 in 88 minutes of actual playing time. Bradman declared, leaving himself nine hours in which to dismiss England. The damp wicket enabled Lindwall and Johnston to make the ball rear up. Further rain interrupted the England second innings. Hutton, for once, was the uncertain opening batsman, whilst Washbrook scored relatively freely. Lindwall had Hutton caught in the slips, then Toshack came on to remove both Edrich and Washbrook. Compton and Dollery carried the total to 106 for three at the close.

Whatever slim hopes England entertained disappeared with the second ball of the last day when Compton was brilliantly caught by Miller at first slip. Resistance virtually disappeared and at 2.22 the game was over.

The press gave the England selectors a drubbing - the fact that Australia had won so easily despite the absence of Miller as a bowler did not go unnoticed.

The attendance was 132,000 with receipts of £43,000.

S.G.Barnes
A duck and a century in the Second Test.

ENGLAND v AUSTRALIA (2nd Test)

Australia

S.G.Barnes	c Hutton b Coxon	0	c Washbrook b Yardley	141
A.R.Morris	c Hutton b Coxon	105	b Wright	62
D.G.Bradman*	c Hutton b Bedser	38	c Edrich b Bedser	89
A.L.Hassett	b Yardley	47	b Yardley	0
K.R.Miller	lbw b Bedser	4	c Bedser b Laker	74
W.A.Brown	lbw b Yardley	24	c Evans b Coxon	32
I.W.Johnson	c Evans b Edrich	4	(8) not out	9
D.Tallon†	c Yardley b Bedser	53		
R.R.Lindwall	b Bedser	15	(7) st Evans b Laker	25
W.A.Johnston	st Evans b Wright	29		
E.R.H.Toshack	not out	20		
Extras	b 3, lb 7, nb 1	11	b 22, lb 5, nb 1	28
Total	(427 mins)	350	(417 mins) 7 wkts dec.	460

Fall of wickets (1): 1-3, 2-87, 3-166, 4-173, 5-216, 6-225, 7-246, 8-275, 9-320, 10-350
Fall of wickets (2): 1-122, 2-296, 3-296, 4-329, 5-416, 6-445, 7-460

England

L.Hutton	b Johnson	20	c Johnson b Lindwall	13
C.Washbrook	c Tallon b Lindwall	8	c Tallon b Toshack	37
W.J.Edrich	b Lindwall	5	c Johnson b Toshack	2
D.C.S.Compton	c Miller b Johnston	53	c Miller b Johnston	29
H.E.Dollery	b Lindwall	0	b Lindwall	37
N.W.D.Yardley*	b Lindwall	44	b Toshack	11
A.Coxon	c and b Johnson	19	lbw b Toshack	0
T.G.Evans†	c Miller b Johnson	9	not out	24
J.C.Laker	c Tallon b Johnson	28	b Lindwall	0
A.V.Bedser	b Lindwall	9	c Hassett b Johnston	9
D.V.P.Wright	not out	13	c Lindwall b Toshack	4
Extras	lb 3, nb 4	7	b 16, lb 4	20
Total	(303 mins)	215	(250 mins)	186

Fall of wickets (1): 1-17, 2-32, 3-46, 4-46, 5-133, 6-134, 7-145, 8-186, 9-197, 10-215
Fall of wickets (2): 1-42, 2-52, 3-65, 4-106, 5-133, 6-133, 7-141, 8-141, 9-158, 10-186

England Bowling

	O	M	R	W		O	M	R	W	
Bedser	43	14	100	4		34	6	112	1	
Coxon	35	10	90	2		28	3	82	1	(1nb)
Edrich	8	0	43	1		2	0	11	0	
Wright	21.3	8	54	1	(1nb)	19	4	69	1	
Laker	7	3	17	0		31,2	6	111	2	
Yardley	15	4	35	2		13	4	36	2	
Compton						3	0	11	0	

Australia Bowling

	O	M	R	W		O	M	R	W	
Lindwall	27.4	7	70	5	(2nb)	23	9	61	3	
Johnston	22	4	43	2	(2nb)	33	15	62	2	
Johnson	35	13	72	3		2	1	3	0	
Toshack	18	11	23	0		20.1	6	40	5	

Umpires: C.N.Woolley and D.Davies
Close of play: 1st day: Australia (1) 258-7 (Tallon 25, Lindwall 3); 2nd day: England (1) 207-9 (Bedser 6, Wright 8); 3rd day: Australia (2) 343-4 (Miller 22, Brown 7); 4th day: England (2) 106-3 (Compton 29, Dollery 21)

A.R.Morris scored 105 in 209 minutes with 1 six and 14 fours. S.G.Barnes scored 141 in 277 minutes with 2 sixes and 14 fours. S.G.Barnes and A.R.Morris added 122 in 120 minutes for the 1st wicket in the second innings. S.G.Barnes and D.G.Bradman added 174 in 155 minutes for the 2nd wicket in the second innings. A.L.Hassett was out 1st ball in the second innings. J.C.Laker was out 2nd ball in the second innings.

SURREY v AUSTRALIANS

Played at The Oval on June 30, July 1, 2 1948
Australians won by 10 wickets
Toss won by Australians

Put in to bat, the county made an indifferent start; Fishlock retired due to a hit on the head from a short ball from Loxton. He had made 2 and the score was only 8. (He returned at the fall of the fourth wicket.) Squires and Barton both fell cheaply to Loxton. Parker was the only batsman to flourish. At the wicket about three hours he scored mainly through drives and pulls. Although Australia lost Hamence to the first ball of the innings - he opened in place of Brown, who had split a finger whilst attempting to catch Fishlock - Bradman and Hassett soon had the runs flowing in the absence of Alec Bedser. Runs came so fast that the pair added 147 in the final 90 minutes of the first day.

The best part of another hundred were made on the second morning before Surrey finally took the second wicket. Bradman hit 15 fours and scored his runs in 141 minutes. Hassett batted three hours and hit 10 fours. Fishlock made a bright start to Surrey's second innings, reaching 61 in 85 minutes. Parker and Holmes added 107 for the 7th wicket. Needing 122 to win the Australians did what they liked with the bowling and victory came in less than an hour.

SURREY v AUSTRALIANS

Surrey

L.B.Fishlock	c McCool b Hamence	31	st Saggers b McCool	61
D.G.W.Fletcher	c Hassett b Toshack	26	st Saggers b McCool	18
H.S.Squires	c Bradman b Loxton	0	c Toshack b McCool	13
M.R.Barton	c Ring b Loxton	4	c Miller b Loxton	18
J.F.Parker	lbw b Ring	76	c McCool b Ring	81
A.J.W.McIntyre†	lbw b Ring	6	b Toshack	11
E.A.Bedser	c Saggers b Hamence	0	st Saggers b Toshack	3
E.R.T.Holmes*	c Harvey b Toshack	23	st Saggers b McCool	54
B.Constable	run out	2	b McCool	4
E.A.Watts	b Ring	30	not out	1
W.S.Surridge	not out	4	c sub (Johnson) b McCool	12
Extras	b 9, lb 7, nb 3	19	b 9, lb 3, nb 1	13
Total	(240 mins)	221	(280 mins)	289

Fall of wickets (1): 1-8, 2-14, 3-64, 4-85, 5-145, 6-147, 7-180, 8-183, 9-217, 10-221
Fall of wickets (2): 1-44, 2-78, 3-94, 4-128, 5-150, 6-160, 7-267, 8-275, 9-275, 10-289

Australians

A.L.Hassett	c Holmes b Watts	139		
R.A.Hamence	c Parker b Watts	0		
D.G.Bradman*	c Barton b Squires	128		
K.R.Miller	c McIntyre b Surridge	9		
R.N.Harvey	run out	43	(1) not out	73
S.J.E.Loxton	c Surridge b Parker	8	(2) not out	47
C.L.McCool	b Surridge	26		
R.A.Saggers†	b Squires	12		
D.T.Ring	not out	15		
E.R.H.Toshack	lbw b Constable	1		
W.A.Brown	absent injured	0		
Extras	b 5, lb 1, nb 2	8	lb 1, nb 1	2
Total	(281 mins)	389	(57 mins) 0 wkts	122

Fall of wickets (1): 1-6, 2-237, 3-276, 4-289, 5-310, 6-355, 7-362, 8-386, 9-389

Australians Bowling

	O	M	R	W		O	M	R	W	
Loxton	25	7	47	2	(1nb)	18	3	53	1	
Hamence	13	4	24	2		8	0	30	0	
Toshack	20	2	76	2		12	6	29	2	
Miller	1	1	0	0						
Ring	21.2	5	51	3	(2nb)	24	6	51	1	(1nb)
McCool	3	1	4	0		45.5	10	113	6	

Surrey Bowling

	O	M	R	W		O	M	R	W	
Surridge	22	0	123	2	(2nb)	7	1	43	0	(1nb)
Watts	10	0	64	2						
Parker	25	5	62	1		5	0	22	0	
Bedser	20	1	85	0		5	0	23	0	
Constable	7.1	1	23	1		3.1	0	32	0	
Squires	10	2	24	2						

Umpires: G.M.Lee and F.S.Lee
Close of play: 1st day: Australians (1) 153-1 (Hassett 64, Bradman 84); 2nd day: Surrey (2): 173-6 (Parker 33, Holmes 7)

A.L.Hassett scored 139 in 180 minutes with 10 fours. D.G.Bradman scored 128 in 141 minutes with 15 fours.
A.L.Hassett and D.G.Bradman added 231 in 141 minutes for the 2nd wicket in the first innings. J.F.Parker and E.R.T.Holmes added 107 in 90 minutes for the 7th wicket in the second innings. R.N.Harvey and S.J.E.Loxton added an unbroken 122 in 57 minutes for the first wicket in the second innings.

GLOUCESTERSHIRE v AUSTRALIANS

Played at Bristol on July 3, 5, 6 1948
Australians won by an innings and 363 runs
Toss won by Australians

The Australian batsmen continued where they finished in the preceding match. On the first day they hit 560 for five. Morris began the onslaught with a century before lunch and reached 200 before tea. In all he batted five hours, was out with the total 466 and hit 42 fours and a six.

On the second day another 214 runs came in 120 minutes. Loxton hit four sixes and 14 fours. Crapp was decidedly the best of the county batsmen. His hundred came in 192 minutes. Miller still did not bowl and the wickets were mainly taken by the spinners, Johnson's bag being eleven for 100.

A.R.Morris scored 290 in 302 minutes with 1 six and 42 fours. S.J.E.Loxton scored 159 in 176 minutes with 4 sixes and 14 fours. S.G.Barnes and A.R.Morris added 102 in 75 minutes for the first wicket. A.R.Morris and K.R.Miller added 136 in 93 minutes for the 3rd wicket. A.R.Morris and R.N.Harvey added 162 in 88 minutes for the 4th wicket. S.J.E.Loxton and C.L.McCool added 140 in 84 minutes for the 6th wicket. S.J.E.Loxton and I.W.Johnson added 105 in 55 minutes for the 7th wicket. J.F.Crapp scored 100 in 194 minutes with 1 five and 10 fours. T.W.J.Goddard was out 1st ball in the first innings.

GLOUCESTERSHIRE v AUSTRALIANS

Australians

S.G.Barnes	c Crapp b Cook	44
A.R.Morris	c and b Scott	290
A.L.Hassett*	st Wilson b Cook	21
K.R.Miller	c Cook b Scott	51
R.N.Harvey	c Allen b Cook	95
S.J.E.Loxton	not out	159
C.L.McCool	b Barnett	76
I.W.Johnson	c and b Hale	27
R.R.Lindwall	not out	0
R.A.Saggers†	did not bat	
D.T.Ring	did not bat	
Extras	b 4, lb 6, w 1	11
Total	(482 mins) 7 wkts dec.	774

Fall of wickets: 1-102, 2-168, 3-304, 4-466, 5-529, 6-669, 7-774

Gloucestershire

G.M.Emmett	c Lindwall b Johnson	43	b Ring	9
B.O.Allen*	c and b Johnson	31	c Harvey b Johnson	34
C.J.Barnett	c Lindwall b Ring	10	b Ring	4
J.F.Crapp	not out	100	c Saggers b Johnson	32
C.I.Monks	b Ring	1	c Harvey b Johnson	5
A.E.Wilson†	c Barnes b Loxton	46	b Ring	10
I.E.Hale	b Johnson	3	c Ring b Johnson	4
L.M.Cranfield	lbw b Morris	23	c Morris b Ring	1
C.J.Scott	st Saggers b Johnson	2	st Saggers b Ring	3
T.W.J.Goddard	c Saggers b Johnson	0	not out	10
C.Cook	b Johnson	5	st Saggers b Johnson	13
Extras	b 9, lb 5, nb 1	15	b 4, lb 3	7
Total	(273 mins)	279	(175 mins)	132

Fall of wickets (1): 1-74, 2-79, 3-87, 4-90, 5-175, 6-187, 7-257, 8-267, 9-267, 10-279
Fall of wickets (2): 1-16, 2-20, 3-72, 4-80, 5-93, 6-100, 7-101, 8-109, 9-109, 10-132

Gloucestershire Bowling

	O	M	R	W	
Barnett	24	2	102	1	
Scott	31	2	172	2	
Monks	9	1	32	0	
Goddard	32	3	186	0	
Cook	41	6	147	3	
Cranfield	23	4	106	0	
Hale	3	0	18	1	(1w)

Australians Bowling

	O	M	R	W		O	M	R	W
Lindwall	18	4	36	0		3	1	5	0
Loxton	9	2	22	1		2	0	2	0
Johnson	31.4	12	68	6		17.1	6	32	5
Ring	25	3	83	2	(1nb)	25	9	47	5
McCool	10	0	35	0		9	5	16	0
Morris	4	0	20	1		9	3	15	0
Hassett						2	0	8	0

Umpires: F.S.Lee and K.McCanlis
Close of play: 1st day: Australians 560-5 (Loxton 46, McCool 8); 2nd day: Gloucestershire (1) 261-7 (Crapp 91, Scott 0)

ENGLAND v AUSTRALIA (3rd Test)

Played at Old Trafford, Manchester on July 8, 9, 10, 12 (no play), 13 1948
Match drawn
Toss won by England

The England selectors made the controversial decision to drop Hutton, who was replaced by Emmett of Gloucestershire. Young came in for Wright, Pollard for Coxon and Crapp for Laker, thus increasing the batting strength. Wardle was 12th man. The Australians introduced Loxton for Brown, Harvey yet again being 12th man.

Yardley won the toss. He decided to bat on a green wicket. Lindwall and Johnston produced some lively bowling and both openers perished. Edrich seemed completely at sea, although he had made a hundred in the county match just completed. Compton was hit a painful blow on the elbow by Lindwall and had scarcely recovered when he mishit a no-ball from the same bowler, which deflected off the edge of his bat on to his forehead. He retired hurt having made 4 with the score on 33. Crapp now had to make his Test debut. England went completely on the defensive and by lunch were 57 for two. On the resumption Crapp played some attacking shots, including hitting Johnson for six, but Lindwall put a stop to his progress, trapping him leg before. Two more wickets - those of Dollery and Edrich - soon followed. Compton resumed his innings with the total on 119 for five. He received support from Yardley and a more robust response from Evans. Compton and Evans added 75 in 70 minutes, though the Kent wicketkeeper was out before the close when the score was 231 for seven.

Compton and Bedser occupied the crease right through until lunch on the second day, the score at that point being 323 for seven - Compton 113, Bedser 37. Compton collected 3 fours directly after lunch, but then stupidly ran out Bedser. Pollard came in, took a tremendous hoick at the ball and propelled the missile straight into the ribs of Barnes fielding at silly mid-on. Barnes went down like a felled log. There was much sympathy for him as he was carried off by four policemen, but his suicide short leg fielding invited disaster. The last two wickets did not take long and Compton carried out his bat. His 145 had lasted 5 hours and 27 minutes and contained 16 fours.

Johnson opened the batting with Morris, since Barnes was unfit. The emergency opener soon went caught behind. Bradman arrived and to the hysterical delight of the partisan crowd was quickly dismissed by Pollard. Morris and Hassett saw off the quick bowlers and seemed set for a long stand, when Hassett tried to drive Young, mistimed the shot and was caught at cover.

The ground was full early on Saturday morning. The sun shone and the boundary rope appeared to have been moved in to accommodate the crush. Miller looked unhappy, played some indiscreet shots and departed, leg before to Pollard. Barnes came in but was clearly unwell - in fact he had collapsed in the nets earlier. After 30 minutes and one run, he collapsed again and was helped back to the dressing room - the score being 139 for four. Morris went soon afterwards and though Loxton played confidently, the Australians were all out for 221.

Lindwall dismissed Emmett with the first ball he bowled to him. Miller, who, despite his injury was called on to open the bowling with Lindwall, bowled even faster than his colleague and beat Washbrook, but just missed the stumps. Bouncers were the order of the day. The umpire no-balled Lindwall for dragging, which seemed to incense the bowler. Washbrook tried his favourite hook, sending the ball straight to Hassett at deep fine leg - Hassett dropped the catch. Edrich and Washbrook gained the upper hand. The pair added 124, both batsmen had exceeded fifty and all seemed to be going England's way, when Washbrook ran out Edrich, a sharp return by Morris hitting the stumps. Compton, the hero of the first innings, came and went, caught in the slips. At stumps Washbrook was 85 not out - he had been missed three times, twice by Hassett and once by Johnson.

21,000 people turned up at Old Trafford for Monday's play: not a ball was bowled.

There was so much rain that the match did not recommence until 2.15 on Tuesday. Yardley declared, but the pitch was slow and of little help to the bowlers. It was soon apparent that a draw was the only outcome. Young had Johnson caught, then Bradman and Morris employed dead-bat tactics and the game came gently to an end.

The total attendance of 133,740 included those poor souls who watched Monday's rain.

D. Tallon
First choice wicket-keeper

D.T.Ring
Limited opportunity in the Tests.
He took 60 first-class wickets
on the tour.

ENGLAND v AUSTRALIA (3rd Test)

England

Batsman	Dismissal (1)		Dismissal (2)	
C.Washbrook	b Johnston	11	not out	85
G.M.Emmett	c Barnes b Lindwall	10	c Tallon b Lindwall	0
W.J.Edrich	c Tallon b Lindwall	32	run out	53
D.C.S.Compton	not out	145	c Miller b Toshack	0
J.F.Crapp	lbw b Lindwall	37	not out	19
H.E.Dollery	b Johnston	1		
N.W.D.Yardley*	c Johnson b Toshack	22		
T.G.Evans†	c Johnston b Lindwall	34		
A.V.Bedser	run out	37		
R.Pollard	b Toshack	3		
J.A.Young	c Bradman b Johnston	4		
Extras	b 7, lb 17, nb 3	27	b 9, lb 7, w 1	17
Total	(570 mins)	363	(208 mins) 3 wkts dec.	174

Fall of wickets (1): 1-22, 2-28, 3-96, 4-97, 5-119, 6-141, 7-216, 8-337, 9-352, 10-363
Fall of wickets (2): 1-1, 2-125, 3-129

Australia

Batsman	Dismissal (1)		Dismissal (2)	
A.R.Morris	c Compton b Bedser	51	not out	54
I.W.Johnson	c Evans b Bedser	1	c Crapp b Young	6
D.G.Bradman*	lbw b Pollard	7	not out	30
A.L.Hassett	c Washbrook b Young	38		
K.R.Miller	lbw b Pollard	31		
S.G.Barnes	retired hurt	1		
S.J.E.Loxton	b Pollard	36		
D.Tallon†	c Evans b Edrich	18		
R.R.Lindwall	c Washbrook b Bedser	23		
W.A.Johnston	c Crapp b Bedser	3		
E.R.H.Toshack	not out	0		
Extras	b 5, lb 4, nb 3	12	nb 2	2
Total	(308 mins)	221	(160 mins) 1 wkt	92

Fall of wickets (1): 1-3, 2-13, 3-82, 4-135, 5-139, 6-172, 7-208, 8-219, 9-221
Fall of wickets (2): 1-10

Australia Bowling

	O	M	R	W		O	M	R	W	
Lindwall	40	8	99	4	(3nb)	14	4	37	1	
Johnston	45.5	13	67	3		14	3	34	0	
Loxton	7	0	18	0		8	2	29	0	
Toshack	41	20	75	2		12	5	26	1	
Johnson	38	16	77	0		7	3	16	0	
Miller						14	7	15	0	(1w)

England Bowling

	O	M	R	W		O	M	R	W	
Bedser	36	12	81	4	(2nb)	19	12	27	0	(1nb)
Pollard	32	9	53	3	(1nb)	10	8	6	0	
Edrich	7	3	27	1		2	0	8	0	
Yardley	4	0	12	0						
Young	14	5	36	1		21	12	31	1	
Compton						9	3	18	0	(1nb)

Umpires: D.Davies and F.Chester
Close of play: 1st day: England (1) 231-7 (Compton 64, Bedser 4); 2nd day: Australia (1) 126-3 (Morris 48, Miller 23); 3rd day: England (2) 174-3 (Washbrook 85, Crapp 19); 4th day: no play

D.C.S.Comption scored 145 in 327 minutes with 16 fours. D.C.S.Compton and A.V.Bedser added 121 in 150 minutes for the 8th wicket in the first innings. C.Washbrook and W.J.Edrich added 124 in 136 minutes for the 2nd wicket in the second innings.

MIDDLESEX v AUSTRALIANS

Played at Lord's on July 17, 19, 20 1948
Australians won by 10 wickets
Toss won by Middlesex

After his second innings failure in the Test, Compton returned to the fray for Middlesex and held the county's first innings together with 62 made in about 135 minutes. No one else made any substantial contribution and when rain ended the first day's play at 5 o'clock, the Australians were 6 for no wicket.

Whitcombe took two quick wickets on the Monday, and the young leg-spinner Bedford dismissed Harvey, but Morris and Loxton went for the runs and their partnership of 172 came in less than two hours. The county attack was hampered because Whitcombe retired with a strained leg, not bowling after lunch.

At the tea interval on the second day, King George VI and Queen Elizabeth, who had come to watch the afternoon's play, met the players.

Sims took three wickets in an over, and brought the Australian innings to a rather abrupt end. The county lost four vital wickets in the late afternoon of Monday; in addition Robertson was hit in the face by a short-pitched no-ball from Lindwall and retired hurt when the score was 27 for three.

Dewes and Leslie Compton shared in a bright sixth wicket partnership of 73 on the last morning; this however could do no more than postpone the inevitable.

MIDDLESEX v AUSTRALIANS

Middlesex

J.D.B.Robertson	b Johnston	2	retired hurt		19
S.M.Brown	c Morris b Ring	39	b Johnston		3
W.J.Edrich	c Tallon b Johnston	27	lbw b Lindwall		1
D.C.S.Compton	b Loxton	62	lbw b Johnston		2
J.G.Dewes	c Tallon b Johnston	4	b McCool		51
F.G.Mann*	c McCool b Lindwall	15	b Lindwall		0
L.H.Compton†	c Lindwall b Loxton	17	(8) c and b McCool		38
J.M.Sims	c and b Loxton	1	(7) c Loxton b Ring		7
P.A.Whitcombe	not out	5	c Lindwall b McCool		8
J.A.Young	st Tallon b McCool	14	b Loxton		0
P.I.Bedford	b McCool	0	not out		1
Extras	b 6, lb 10, nb 1	17	b 1, lb 3, nb 1		5
Total	(260 mins)	203	(140 mins)		135

Fall of wickets (1): 1-13, 2-78, 3-81, 4-92, 5-144, 6-182, 7-183, 8-188, 9-203, 10-203
Fall of wickets (2): 1-15, 2-16, 3-27, 4-27, 5-40, 6-113, 7-132, 8-133, 9-135

Australians

W.A.Brown	lbw b Whitcombe	8		
A.R.Morris	c Brown b Young	109		
D.G.Bradman*	c D.C.S.Compton b Whitcombe	6		
R.N.Harvey	c Mann b Bedford	10		
S.J.E.Loxton	c Edrich b Sims	123		
R.A.Hamence	lbw b Sims	30		
C.L.McCool	c Young b Sims	0	(1) not out	7
R.R.Lindwall	st L.H.Compton b Sims	1		
D.Tallon†	b Sims	17		
D.T.Ring	b Sims	2	(2) not out	15
W.A.Johnston	not out	6		
Extras	b 1, lb 3, nb 1	5		
Total	(303 mins)	317	(10 mins) 0 wkts	22

Fall of wickets (1): 1-14, 2-28, 3-53, 4-225, 5-271, 6-271, 7-272, 8-296, 9-298, 10-317

Australians Bowling

	O	M	R	W		O	M	R	W	
Lindwall	16	3	28	1		9	2	31	2	(1nb)
Johnston	20	3	43	3	(1nb)	12	4	28	2	
Loxton	21	5	33	3		7	2	15	1	
McCool	18	6	54	2		10.4	3	27	3	
Ring	13	4	28	1		7	0	29	1	

Middlesex Bowling

	O	M	R	W		O	M	R	W	
Whitcombe	13	2	43	2						
Edrich	20	2	59	0						
Bedford	11	3	44	1		2	0	11	0	
Young	36	13	78	1						
Sims	24	2	65	6	(1nb)	2	0	11	0	
D.C.S.Compton	3	0	23	0						

Umpires: H.G.Baldwin and E.Cooke
Close of play: 1st day: Australians (1) 6-0 (Brown 5, Morris 1); 2nd day: Middlesex (2) 36-4 (Dewes 6, Sims 3)

A.R.Morris scored 109 in 195 minutes with 17 fours. S.J.E.Loxton scored 123 in 147 minutes with 16 fours.
A.R.Morris and S.J.E.Loxton added 172 in 117 minutes for the 4th wicket in the first innings. I.Bedford was out
1st ball in the first innings. F.G.Mann was out 1st ball in the second innings having come in when Robertson
retired hurt.

ENGLAND v AUSTRALIA (4th Test)

Played at Headingley, Leeds on July 22, 23, 24, 26, 27 1948
Australia won by 7 wickets
Toss won by England

Hutton was reinstated in place of Emmett who was 12th man, Laker replaced Young and Cranston came in for Dollery. Barnes and Tallon were unfit, so Australia's new faces were Harvey and Saggers, Brown being 12th man.

Yardley won the toss and took first use of an ideal batting strip. Hutton and Washbrook determined to forego all risk and the famous Washbrook hook was definitely left in the pavilion. Runs came in singles. The opening partnership, which was twice briefly adjourned for rain, added 168. Washbrook went on to his 100 in 230 minutes and was out just before the close. Bedser came in as nightwatchman. The Australian bowling was poor, the pitch not suiting the pace of Lindwall and Miller.

England needed to score fast on the second morning, but the light was poor and the runs came very slowly. In thirty minutes 4 runs were made. Then Bedser, rather than Edrich, began to open up; by lunch the total was 360 for two with Edrich 76 and Bedser 52. Bradman in desperation even brought Morris on to bowl. Johnson caught and bowled Bedser to break the partnership. Bedser had batted 177 minutes and hit 2 sixes and 8 fours. To win the Ashes, England needed victory. The remaining batsmen therefore had to score quickly; they attempted this and failed, so the all out total of 496 was not as high as Australia feared.

Australia were 63 for one overnight. Bradman had received a tremendous reception on going out to bat, but on the third morning Pollard dealt what appeared to be a mortal blow to Australia's hopes. He made a delivery rear up unexpectedly; Hassett was unable to get his bat out of the way and sent a catch to Crapp. Bradman saw what had happened to Hassett and was prepared for another similar delivery, but the ball skidded through and clean bowled him. The total was now 68 for three. Harvey arrived; it must have been a daunting experience for the young batsman. Miller however showed him what could be done and the pair had added more than 100 when the next wicket, Miller caught trying to hit Yardley out of the ground, fell. In about 90 minutes the pair had put on 121. Loxton continued where Miller left off and a further century partnership came almost as quickly. Harvey hit 17 fours. He completed three figures and virtually threw his wicket away. Loxton was still going too well for England. Yardley brought himself back and for the second time removed a batsman in full flow. Lindwall took on the principal role. He batted well and with the aid of Johnston and Toshack, the latter batting with a runner due to the recurrence of his knee injury, continued the innings into the fourth day and what was more important within sight of the England total.

The ground was again filled to capacity for Monday, the crowd reducing the playing area even further than on the previous days. The total attendance for the match was 158,000, a new English record, with receipts of £34,000.

Hutton and Washbrook gave England a splendid start to their second innings. A running catch by Harvey on the boundary removed Washbrook - his fatal hook again. Immediately afterwards Hutton fell to another running catch, this time taken by Bradman. Edrich and Compton were very subdued in the early stages of their stand of 103. At tea England were 209 for two. The middle order went in quick succession, then Evans and Laker stayed to the close.

Yardley batted on for two overs of the fifth morning, which gave him the opportunity of selecting the roller - the heaviest roller would assist the task of making the pitch crumble. Australia required 404 in 344 minutes. After only three overs, Yardley brought on his single specialist spinner, Laker. The first 45 minutes produced just 32 runs. Compton was introduced into the attack and in his second over saw Evans drop Morris: it was to prove an expensive error. Compton did however take a brilliant catch just off the ground to remove Hassett; 57 for one in 75 minutes. Yardley tried Hutton's leg-breaks, but there was no length to them. Compton bowled a beautiful over which confused Bradman and had the great batsman dropped in the slips by Crapp. At lunch the total was 121 for one. Both Morris and Bradman had one or two more lucky escapes; runs were coming very fast in between the errors and by tea only 112 runs were required in 105 minutes. Morris was at last dismissed by Yardley; Miller tried to finish the game in half a dozen hits. It was left to Harvey to score the winning boundary. Morris hit 33 fours, Bradman 29. The game was over fifteen minutes early. It was a remarkable feat by Australia, but England did nothing to help themselves by their poor out-cricket and the lack of a second specialist spin bowler.

W.A.Johnston
27 wickets in the Test series at 23.33

C.Washbrook scored 143 in 317 minutes with 22 fours. W.J.Edrich scored 111 in 314 minutes with 1 six and 13 fours. L. Hutton and C.Washbrook added 168 in 195 minutes for the 1st wicket in the first innings. W.J.Edrich and A.V.Bedser added 155 in 177 minutes for the 3rd wicket in the first innings. R.N.Harvey scored 112 in 188 minutes with 17 fours. K.R.Miller and R.N.Harvey added 121 in 97 minutes for the 4th wicket in the first innings. R.N.Harvey and S.J.E.Loxton added 105 in 92 minutes for the 5th wicket in the first innings. L.Hutton and C.Washbrook added 129 in 146 minutes for the 1st wicket in the second innings. W.J.Edrich and D.C.S. Compton added 103 in 93 minutes for the 3rd wicket in the second innings. A.R.Morris scored 182 in 281 minutes with 33 fours. D.G.Bradman scored 173 in 255 minutes with 29 fours. A.R.Morris and D.G.Bradman added 301 in 217 minutes for the 2nd wicket in the second innings.

ENGLAND v AUSTRALIA (4th Test)

England

L.Hutton	b Lindwall	81	c Bradman b Johnson		57
C.Washbrook	c Lindwall b Johnston	143	c Harvey b Johnston		65
W.J.Edrich	c Morris b Johnson	111	lbw b Lindwall		54
A.V.Bedser	c and b Johnson	79	(9) c Hassett b Miller		17
D.C.S.Compton	c Saggers b Lindwall	23	(4) c Miller b Johnston		66
J.F.Crapp	b Toshack	5	(5) b Lindwall		18
N.W.D.Yardley*	b Miller	25	(6) c Harvey b Johnston		7
K.Cranston	b Loxton	10	(7) c Saggers b Johnston		0
T.G.Evans†	c Hassett b Loxton	3	(8) not out		47
J.C.Laker	c Saggers b Loxton	4	not out		15
R.Pollard	not out	0			
Extras	b 2, lb 8, w 1, nb 1	12	b 4, lb 12, nb 3		19
Total	(595 mins)	496	(342 mins) 8 wkts dec.		365

Fall of wickets (1): 1-168, 2-268, 3-423, 4-426, 5-447, 6-473, 7-486, 8-490, 9-496, 10-496
Fall of wickets (2): 1-129, 2-129, 3-232, 4-260, 5-277, 6-278, 7-293, 8-330

Australia

A.L.Hassett	c Crapp b Pollard	13	c and b Compton		17
A.R.Morris	c Cranston b Bedser	6	c Pollard b Yardley		182
D.G.Bradman*	b Pollard	33	not out		173
K.R.Miller	c Edrich b Yardley	58	lbw b Cranston		12
R.N.Harvey	b Laker	112	not out		4
S.J.E.Loxton	b Yardley	93			
I.W.Johnson	c Cranston b Laker	10			
R.R.Lindwall	c Crapp b Bedser	77			
R.A.Saggers†	st Evans b Laker	5			
W.A.Johnston	c Edrich b Bedser	13			
E.R.H.Toshack	not out	12			
Extras	b 9, lb 14, nb 3	26	b 6, lb 9, nb 1		16
Total	(435 mins)	458	(328 mins) 3 wkts		404

Fall of wickets (1): 1-13, 2-65, 3-68, 4-189, 5-294, 6-329, 7-344, 8-355, 9-403, 10-458
Fall of wickets (2): 1-57, 2-358, 3-396

Australia Bowling

	O	M	R	W		O	M	R	W	
Lindwall	38	10	79	2		26	6	84	2	
Miller	17.1	2	43	1		21	5	53	1	
Johnston	38	13	86	1	(1nb,1w)	29	5	95	4	(3nb)
Toshack	35	6	112	1						
Loxton	26	4	55	3		10	2	29	0	
Johnson	33	9	89	2		21	2	85	1	
Morris	5	0	20	0						

England Bowling

	O	M	R	W		O	M	R	W	
Bedser	31.2	4	92	3	(2nb)	21	2	56	0	(1nb)
Pollard	38	6	104	2	(1nb)	22	6	55	0	
Cranston	14	1	51	0		7.1	0	28	1	
Edrich	3	0	19	0						
Laker	30	8	113	3		32	11	93	0	
Yardley	17	6	38	2		13	1	44	1	
Compton	3	0	15	0		15	3	82	1	
Hutton						4	1	30	0	

Umpires: F.Chester and H.G.Baldwin
Close of play: 1st day: England (1) 268-2 (Edrich 41, Bedser 0); 2nd day: Australia (1) 63-1 (Hassett 13, Bradman 31); 3rd day: Australia (1) 457-9 (Lindwall 76, Toshack 12); 4th day: England (2) 362-8 (Evans 47, Laker 14)

DERBYSHIRE v AUSTRALIANS

Played at Derby on July 28, 29, 30 1948
Australians won by an innings and 34 runs
Toss won by Australians

17,000, a Derbyshire record, turned up to watch the first day's play. Barnes re-appeared in the Australian side, but the county lacked both Copson and Pope. Brown batted with great care in the first part of his innings, taking three hours to reach fifty; his remaining 90 came in less than 120 minutes and in all he hit 16 fours.

Elliott batted stubbornly in Derbyshire's first innings, but the bowling was not too formidable. Over 200 behind, the home side were invited to follow on and this time McCool, who had been unable to find a length in the first innings, bowled very accurately. Townsend and Smith added three figures for the second wicket, but as soon as McCool had Townsend leg before, no one was capable of partnering Smith and the innings fell apart.

DERBYSHIRE v AUSTRALIANS

Australians

S.G.Barnes	b Gladwin	24
W.A.Brown	c Gladwin b Gothard	140
D.G.Bradman*	b Gothard	62
K.R.Miller	lbw b Jackson	57
R.N.Harvey	c Elliott b Rhodes	32
R.A.Hamence	st Dawkes b Gothard	21
S.J.E.Loxton	c Revill b Jackson	51
C.L.McCool	c Smith b Rhodes	31
R.A.Saggers†	not out	6
D.T.Ring	b Jackson	4
W.A.Johnston	b Jackson	0
Extras	b 21, lb 5, w 1, nb 1	28
Total	(385 mins)	456

Fall of wickets: 1-11, 2-134, 3-259, 4-314, 5-344, 6-362, 7-431, 8-446, 9-452, 10-456

Derbyshire

C.S.Elliott	lbw b Miller	57	(2) c Miller b Loxton	4	
A.F.Townsend	c Saggers b Miller	0	(1) lbw b McCool	46	
D.Smith	b Miller	11	b McCool	88	
A.C.Revill	c Barnes b Johnston	41	st Saggers b McCool	0	
P.Vaulkhard	c Hamence b Ring	36	lbw b McCool	2	
F.E.Marsh	c Saggers b Johnston	17	b Johnston	7	
G.O.Dawkes†	b Johnston	4	c Johnston b McCool	8	
E.J.Gothard*	not out	26	(10) not out	1	
C.Gladwin	c Loxton b Ring	5	b Loxton	0	
A.E.R.Rhodes	lbw b Ring	14	(8) c Bradman b McCool	4	
H.L.Jackson	b Loxton	6	b Loxton	0	
Extras	b 5, lb 9, w 4, nb 5	23	b 10, lb 4, w 5, nb 3	22	
Total	(260 mins)	240	(227 mins)	182	

Fall of wickets (1): 1-1, 2-26, 3-90, 4-145, 5-176, 6-180, 7-189, 8-199, 9-219, 10-240
Fall of wickets (2): 1-10, 2-110, 3-110, 4-116, 5-151, 6-163, 7-169, 8-175, 9-181, 10-182

Derbyshire Bowling

	O	M	R	W	
Jackson	34.4	4	103	4	
Gladwin	33	6	107	1	(1w)
Rhodes	30	2	99	2	
Gothard	22	0	108	3	(1nb)
Smith	2	0	11	0	
Marsh	1	1	0	0	

Australians Bowling

	O	M	R	W		O	M	R	W	
Miller	16	2	31	3	(2w)	2	0	3	0	
Johnston	22	5	41	3	(3nb,2w)	18	3	35	1	(3nb,3w)
Ring	24	5	73	3	(2nb)	6	1	23	0	
Loxton	17.4	3	27	1		13.4	4	16	3	(2w)
McCool	11	2	45	0		29	8	77	6	
Barnes						14	8	6	0	

Umpires: J.A.Smart and A.Lockett
Close of play: 1st day: Australians 431-7 (Loxton 39); 2nd day: Derbyshire (2) 34-1 (Townsend 16, Smith 6)

W.A.Brown scored 140 in 295 minutes with 16 fours. W.A.Brown and D.G.Bradman added 123 in 124 minutes for the 2nd wicket. W.A.Brown and K.R.Miller added 125 in 75 minutes for the 3rd wicket. A.F.Townsend and D.Smith added 100 in 116 minutes for the 2nd wicket in the second innings. A.F.Townsend was out to the fifth ball of the first innings.

GLAMORGAN v AUSTRALIANS

Played at Swansea on July 31, August 2, 3 (no play) 1948
Match drawn
Toss won by Glamorgan

The Glamorgan side opened with a useful partnership between Davies and Clift; the only other county batsman to prosper was Jones and a total of 192 was not one to worry the tourists.

Miller, with 5 sixes and 7 fours, did what he liked with the bowling on the second morning; Hassett also batted well. At 3 o'clock torrential rain stopped play and the game came to a disappointing end, especially as a huge crowd had turned up on the Bank Holiday Monday. There was no play on the last day.

GLAMORGAN v AUSTRALIANS

Glamorgan

D.E.Davies	lbw b Ring	24
P.B.Clift	c Barnes b Johnson	30
W.G.A.Parkhouse	lbw b Miller	1
W.E.Jones	c Tallon b Johnson	40
W.Wooller*	b Ring	9
A.J.Watkins	lbw b Lindwall	19
L.B.Muncer	c Brown b Lindwall	2
J.T.Eaglestone	b Miller	3
H.G.Davies†	st Tallon b Ring	18
W.M.S.Trick	not out	7
J.C.Clay	st Tallon b Johnson	16
Extras	b 19, lb 6, nb 3	28
Total	(235 mins)	197

Fall of wickets: 1-53, 2-54, 3-85, 4-100, 5-139, 6-141, 7-152, 8-173, 9-177, 10-197

Australians

S.G.Barnes	lbw b Watkins	31
W.A.Brown	c Parkhouse b Wooller	16
A.L.Hassett*	not out	71
K.R.Miller	c Eaglestone b Clay	84
R.N.Harvey	not out	9
R.A.Hamence	did not bat	
I.W.Johnson	did not bat	
C.L.McCool	did not bat	
D.Tallon†	did not bat	
R.R.Lindwall	did not bat	
D.T.Ring	did not bat	
Extras	b 4	4
Total	(218 mins) 3 wkts	215

Fall of wickets: 1-27, 2-67, 3-193

Australians Bowling

	O	M	R	W	
Lindwall	17	4	36	2	
Miller	25	12	41	2	
Johnson	28.4	12	58	3	
Ring	13	6	34	3	(3nb)

Glamorgan Bowling

	O	M	R	W
Wooller	22	3	65	1
Watkins	17	3	47	1
Trick	11	4	37	0
Muncer	15	4	41	0
Jones	3	0	10	0
Clay	5.3	1	11	1

Umpires: J.T.Bell and K.McCanlis

Close of play: 1st day: Australians 44-1 (Barnes 32, Hassett 6); 2nd day: Australians 215-3 (Hassett 71, Harvey 9)

A.L.Hasset and K.R.Miller added 126 in 100 minutes for the 3rd wicket.

WARWICKSHIRE v AUSTRALIANS

Played at Edgbaston, Birmingham on August 4, 5, 6 1948
Australians won by 9 wickets
Toss won by Australians

Put in to bat on a damp pitch, none of the Warwickshire batsmen could master the Australian attack. When the tourists batted, the leg-break bowler, Hollies, bowled himself into the England team for the final Test, taking eight for 107, the best bowling performance against the tourists. An unusual feature of the Australian scorecard was that both opening batsmen, Brown and Morris, were out hit wicket to Hollies. Hassett saved the tourists with an innings of 68 made in 150 minutes and Lindwall hit out to provide a comfortable lead on first innings.

McCool followed Hollies' example in Warwickshire's second innings and helped by Johnston had the match almost sewn up at the close of the second day: the tourists won by nine wickets before lunch on the third morning.

The attendance was 37,893.

WARWICKSHIRE v AUSTRALIANS

Warwickshire

J.R.Thompson	c McCool b Loxton	17	c and b McCool	35
K.A.Taylor	c McCool b Loxton	10	c McCool b Lindwall	0
J.S.Ord	st Saggers b Johnson	6	b Johnston	24
M.P.Donnelly	b Johnston	28	c and b McCool	6
H.E.Dollery	lbw b Lindwall	2	run out	24
A.H.Kardar	c Saggers b Lindwall	4	b Johnston	15
R.H.Maudsley*	c Saggers b Lindwall	0	c Johnson b McCool	9
R.T.Spooner†	b Johnston	20	not out	13
V.H.D.Cannings	not out	18	b Johnston	4
T.L.Pritchard	b Johnson	14	c Bradman b Johnston	0
W.E.Hollies	lbw b Johnson	5	c Loxton b McCool	5
Extras	b 12, lb 2	14	b 16, lb 4	20
Total	(236 mins)	138	(241 mins)	155

Fall of wickets (1): 1-28, 2-29, 3-41, 4-48, 5-52, 6-60, 7-80, 8-111, 9-126, 10-138
Fall of wickets (2): 1-3, 2-39, 3-46, 4-98, 5-98, 6-118, 7-132, 8-147, 9-149, 10-155

Australians

W.A.Brown	hit wkt b Hollies	33	lbw b Hollies	7
A.R.Morris	hit wkt b Hollies	32	not out	20
D.G.Bradman*	b Hollies	31	not out	13
A.L.Hassett	lbw b Hollies	68		
R.N.Harvey	b Hollies	0		
S.J.E.Loxton	lbw b Kardar	0		
C.L.McCool	c Donnelly b Kardar	19		
R.R.Lindwall	c Maudsley b Hollies	45		
I.W.Johnson	not out	13		
R.A.Saggers†	b Hollies	0		
W.A.Johnston	b Hollies	6		
Extras	b 3, lb 4	7	lb 1	1
Total	(279 mins)	254	(35 mins) 1 wkt	41

Fall of wickets (1): 1-50, 2-87, 3-116, 4-116, 5-117, 6-161, 7-231, 8-236, 9-236, 10-254
Fall of wickets (2): 1-18

Australians Bowling

	O	M	R	W	O	M	R	W
Lindwall	16	5	27	3	12	2	32	1
Johnston	22	9	41	2	39	23	32	4
Johnson	22.3	12	29	3	1	1	0	0
Loxton	19	8	27	2	6	0	15	0
McCool					27.5	6	56	4

Warwickshire Bowling

	O	M	R	W	O	M	R	W
Pritchard	16	4	35	0	2	0	7	0
Cannings	10	2	30	0	3	1	6	0
Hollies	43.5	8	107	8	4	0	17	1
Kardar	32	11	75	2	2.4	0	10	0

Umpires: H.Cruice and H.G.Baldwin
Close of play: 1st day: Australians (1) 90-2 (Bradman 20, Hassett 3); 2nd day: Warwickshire (2) 90-3 (Thompson 33, Dollery 18)

R.N.Harvey was out 1st ball. R.A.Saggers was out 2nd ball.

LANCASHIRE v AUSTRALIANS

Played at Old Trafford, Manchester on August 7, 9, 10 1948
Match drawn
Toss won by Australians

The Lancashire Club generously allowed Washbrook to use this fixture for his benefit - when all donations were gathered in, he created a new record of £14,000. Without any outstanding individual innings, the tourists topped 300. The county batsmen really struggled against the pace of Lindwall, Miller and Loxton. Washbrook made a brave 38, but was hit on the right thumb by Lindwall and the injury proved so painful that he was unavailable for the Fifth Test.

In order to make certain the match went into the third day, Bradman did not enforce the follow on; instead he took the opportunity of entertaining the crowd with an innings of 133 in 216 minutes with 17 fours. The declaration did not come until mid-afternoon on the last day, leaving Lancashire with 165 minutes batting. A draw seemed the only possible result, but when the second new ball was due Lindwall dismissed Ikin and Pollard with successive balls and with Washbrook unable to bat, Lancashire just saved the game.

LANCASHIRE v AUSTRALIANS

Australians

S.G.Barnes	c Ikin b Roberts	67	c Wilson b Pollard		90
A.R.Morris	c Wilson b Roberts	49	c Place b Pollard		16
D.G.Bradman*	c Wilson b Roberts	28	not out		133
K.R.Miller	lbw b Ikin	24	c Howard b Pollard		11
R.A.Hamence	c and b Roberts	14	not out		10
S.J.E.Loxton	c Edrich b Roberts	2			
R.R.Lindwall	c Wilson b Roberts	17			
I.W.Johnson	c and b Pollard	48			
D.Tallon†	c Pollard b Greenwood	33			
D.T.Ring	not out	17			
E.R.H.Toshack	c Howard b Pollard	2			
Extras	b 16, lb 3, w 1	20	b 4, lb 1		5
Total	(358 mins)	321	(235 mins) 3 wkts dec.		265

Fall of wickets (1): 1-123, 2-128, 3-175, 4-194, 5-200, 6-202, 7-232, 8-295, 9-315, 10-321
Fall of wickets (2): 1-21, 2-188, 3-216

Lancashire

C.Washbrook	c Miller b Lindwall	38			
W.Place	c Ring b Lindwall	5	(1) b Lindwall		11
G.A.Edrich	c Tallon b Lindwall	0	lbw b Ring		25
J.T.Ikin	c Bradman b Loxton	9	b Lindwall		99
A.Wharton	c Bradman b Miller	5	c Tallon b Johnson		1
N.D.Howard	not out	28	(2) b Lindwall		8
K.Cranston*	st Tallon b Ring	18	(6) c Johnson b Ring		16
P.Greenwood	st Tallon b Johnson	3	(7) not out		16
R.Pollard	c Lindwall b Ring	1	(8) b Lindwall		0
W.B.Roberts	c Loxton b Johnson	1	(9) not out		0
A.E.Wilson†	c and b Johnson	4			
Extras	b 13, lb 4, w 1	18	b 10, lb 12, w 1		23
Total	(186 mins)	130	(162 mins) 7 wkts		199

Fall of wickets (1): 1-21, 2-21, 3-42, 4-66, 5-75, 6-108, 7-115, 8-116, 9-122, 10-130
Fall of wickets (2): 1-21, 2-26, 3-70, 4-87, 5-152, 6-191, 7-191

Lancashire Bowling

	O	M	R	W		O	M	R	W
Pollard	27	6	58	2		27	8	58	3
Greenwood	19	4	62	1		13	2	53	0
Cranston	3	0	24	0		8	2	34	0
Wharton	1	0	4	0					
Ikin	39	12	80	1 (1w)		15	3	51	0
Roberts	42	14	73	6		22	4	64	0

Australians Bowling

	O	M	R	W		O	M	R	W
Lindwall	16	3	32	3 (1w)		11	2	27	4
Miller	11	3	22	1		5	1	10	0
Loxton	9	4	11	1		7	2	21	0
Toshack	7	4	17	0					
Ring	11	4	25	2		22	3	88	2 (1w)
Johnson	5	2	5	3		12	6	30	1

Umpires: T.J.Bartley and J.A.Smart
Close of play: 1st day: Australians (1) 272-7 (Johnson 35, Tallon 20); 2nd day: Australians (2) 81-1 (Barnes 39, Bradman 25)

S.G.Barnes and A.R.Morris added 123 in 96 minutes for the 1st wicket in the first innings. D.G.Bradman scored 133 in 216 minutes with 17 fours. S.G.Barnes and D.G.Bradman added 167 in 159 minutes for the 2nd wicket in the second innings. G.A.Edrich was out 2nd ball in the first innings. R.Pollard was out 1st ball in the second innings.

DURHAM v AUSTRALIANS†

Played at Sunderland on August 11, 12 (no play) 1948
Match drawn
Toss won by Australians

17,000 spectators turned out on the first day and saw the Australians rather uncomfortable against the seam bowling of Herbert and Jackson. Miller and McCool hit out and helped by errors in the field, the total rose to 282.

Durham started disastrously, but managed to put some respectability on the scoreboard by the close of play.

Rain prevented any play on the second day.

DURHAM v AUSTRALIANS†

Australians

D.Tallon	b Jackson	1
W.A.Brown	b Jackson	49
R.N.Harvey	c Thompson b Jackson	2
S.J.E.Loxton	b Herbert	15
C.L.McCool	c Jackson b Herbert	64
R.A.Hamence	c Hardy b Jackson	24
K.R.Miller	b Herbert	55
A.L.Hassett*	c Hardy b Jackson	3
I.W.Johnson	c Robertson b Laidlaw	44
R.A.Saggers†	c Austin b Owen	22
D.T.Ring	not out	1
Extras	lb 1, nb 1	2
		—
Total	(253 mins)	282

Fall of wickets: 1-1, 2-3, 3-22, 4-133, 5-133, 6-208, 7-212, 8-226, 9-280, 10-282

Durham

D.G.Harron	c Hassett b Loxton	0
G.Thompson	b Miller	4
S.Robertson	b Ring	2
W.A.Buffham	st Saggers b McCool	19
D.W.Hardy	not out	19
T.K.Jackson	st Saggers b Johnson	23
N.W.Owen	not out	1
W.K.Laidlaw	did not bat	
A.W.Austin†	did not bat	
F.I.Herbert	did not bat	
R.B.Proud*	did not bat	
Extras	b 2, lb 3	5
		—
Total	(80 mins) 5 wkts	73

Fall of wickets: 1-1, 2-5, 3-25, 4-37, 5-72

Durham Bowling

	O	M	R	W	
Herbert	27 `	3	80	3	
Jackson	29	2	76	5	
Owen	14	1	34	1	(1nb)
Laidlaw	16.5	0	90	1	

Australians Bowling

	O	M	R	W
Miller	8	3	17	1
Loxton	6	3	8	1
Ring	7	2	24	1
McCool	9	4	17	1
Johnson	3	1	2	1

Umpires: J.W.Franks and T.R.Nicholson
Clos of play: Durham 73-5 (Hardy 19, Owen 1)

W.A.Brown and C.L.McCool added 111 in 105 minutes for the 4th wicket.

ENGLAND v AUSTRALIA (5th Test)

Played at Kennington Oval on August 14, 16, 17, 18 1948
Australia won by an innings and 149 runs
Toss won by England

The England selectors made further substantial changes for the final Test. Hollies was brought in for Laker; Dewes, the Cambridge blue, replaced the injured Washbrook; Watkins was preferred to Cranston and Young played in place of Pollard. Simpson was reinstated as 12th man. Therefore the deficiency of spin at Leeds was now made up, but it meant that the England selectors had employed 22 players in the five Tests. Both Australia's injured men Barnes and Tallon were now fit and resumed their places, but Toshack was injured so Harvey kept his place. Ring was preferred to Johnson who did duty as 12th man.

Overnight rain water-logged the wicket and when play started at midday Yardley decided to bat. There were arguments afterwards that Yardley ought to have put Australia in, but it was clearly a difficult decision to have to make. Dewes, on his Test debut, went bowled by Miller off the eighth ball of the innings. Edrich lasted slightly longer, caught hooking by Hassett just backward of square. Compton was also caught attempting a hook. Crapp batted twenty minutes. Miller's pre-lunch spell was six overs for 3 runs and two wickets. Yardley was yorked soon after the interval. Watkins, another Test debutant, made some wild gestures with the bat and was then leg before, having previously received a blow on the shoulder from a ball by Lindwall. Evans and Young had their wickets flattened by Lindwall; Bedser came and went with a bat still unmarked. Hutton, all this time, had played quite calmly, but now with only Hollies, the best known rabbit, for company, hit out and then perished to a catch at the wicket.

In complete contrast, the Australian opening batsmen, Morris and Barnes, found no problems with the wicket. By 5.30 the hundred was on the board and no wickets down. Hollies bowled some good leg-breaks and finally had Barnes caught at the wicket. Bradman left the pavilion to a massive reception. He was applauded all the way to the wicket. Yardley then gathered the England players and called for three cheers. It was a moment of complete emotion and too much even for the great master batsman. He was bowled second delivery by Hollies. Bradman's slow walk back to the dressing-room was a scene not easily forgotten. At the close Australia had a lead of 101, with Morris 77 not out.

Morris reached his 100 in 206 minutes. Wickets fell fairly frequently at the other end, but Morris just went his untroubled way. At last he was out - run out by Tallon. He had been batting for 406 minutes and scored 16 fours. Hollies was England's star; he kept an accurate length and plugged away at the off stump, bowling enough googlies to keep the batsmen guessing.

Dewes was not up to bowling of this standard and his short innings ended when he was bowled not offering a stroke to Lindwall. Edrich stayed with Hutton until the close of the second day. The Middlesex man did not survive long on the third morning, and by lunch England were 121 for two. All England's hopes depended on the partnership between Hutton and Compton. The latter was very unfortunate when Lindwall took a remarkable catch in the slips, off Johnston. Hutton was playing well, with some cover drives being quite magnificent. He was the fourth batsman out, caught by Tallon. The remainder put up little fight, though the match did carry through to the fourth day.

Bradman had comprehensively beaten England in his final Test series. Yardley in his speech to the crowd after the match said:
"In saying good-bye to Don we are saying good-bye to the greatest cricketer of all time. He is not only a great cricketer but a great sportsman, on and off the field."

R.R.Lindwall
He took 6-20 in the first innings of the Fifth Test
and overall 27 wickets in the Test series at 19.52 runs each.

ENGLAND v AUSTRALIA (5th Test)

England

L.Hutton	c Tallon b Lindwall	30	(2) c Tallon b Miller	64	
J.G.Dewes	b Miller	1	(1) b Lindwall	10	
W.J.Edrich	c Hassett b Johnston	3	b Lindwall	28	
D.C.S.Compton	c Morris b Lindwall	4	c Lindwall b Johnston	39	
J.F.Crapp	c Tallon b Miller	0	b Miller	9	
N.W.D.Yardley*	b Lindwall	7	c Miller b Johnston	9	
A.J.Watkins	lbw b Johnston	0	c Hassett b Ring	2	
T.G.Evans†	b Lindwall	1	b Lindwall	8	
A.V.Bedser	b Lindwall	0	b Johnston	0	
J.A.Young	b Lindwall	0	not out	3	
W.E.Hollies	not out	0	c Morris b Johnston	0	
Extras	b 6	6	b 9, lb 4, nb 3	16	
Total	(147 mins)	52	(314 mins)	188	

Fall of wickets (1): 1-2, 2-10, 3-17, 4-23, 5-25, 6-42, 7-45, 8-45, 9-47, 10-52
Fall of wickets (2): 1-20, 2-64, 3-125, 4-153, 5-164, 6-167, 7-178, 8-181, 9-188, 10-188

Australia

S.G.Barnes	c Evans b Hollies	61
A.R.Morris	run out	196
D.G.Bradman*	b Hollies	0
A.L.Hassett	lbw b Young	37
K.R.Miller	st Evans b Hollies	5
R.N.Harvey	c Young b Hollies	17
S.J.E.Loxton	c Evans b Edrich	15
R.R.Lindwall	c Edrich b Young	9
D.Tallon†	c Crapp b Hollies	31
D.T.Ring	c Crapp b Bedser	9
W.A.Johnston	not out	0
Extras	b 4, lb 2, nb 3	9
Total	(433 mins)	389

Fall of wickets: 1-117, 2-117, 3-226, 4-243, 5-265, 6-304, 7-332, 8-359, 9-389, 10-389

Australia Bowling

	O	M	R	W		O	M	R	W	
Lindwall	16.1	5	20	6		25	3	50	3	
Miller	8	5	5	2		15	6	22	2	(1nb)
Johnston	16	4	20	2		27.3	12	40	4	
Loxton	2	1	1	0		10	2	16	0	
Ring						28	13	44	1	(2nb)

England Bowling

	O	M	R	W	
Bedser	31.2	9	61	1	(1nb)
Watkins	4	1	19	0	
Young	51	16	118	2	
Hollies	56	14	131	5	(1nb)
Compton	2	0	6	0	(1nb)
Edrich	9	1	38	1	
Yardley	5	1	7	0	

Umpires: D.Davies and H.G.Baldwin
Close of play: 1st day: Australia (1) 153-2 (Morris 77, Hassett 10); 2nd day: England (2) 54-1 (Hutton 19, Edrich 23); 3rd day: England (2) 178-7 (Yardley 2)

A.R.Morris scored 196 in 406 minutes with 16 fours. S.G.Barnes and A.R.Morris added 117 in 126 minutes for the 1st wicket. A.R.Morris and A.L.Hassett added 109 in 134 minutes for the 3rd wicket. W.E.Hollies was out 1st ball in the second innings.

KENT v AUSTRALIANS

Played at Canterbury on August 21, 23 1948
Australians won by an innings and 186 runs
Toss won by Australians

Having beaten England so easily, the tourists had little difficulty in overwhelming Kent. 19,000 spectators turned out on the first day - a record for Canterbury, but on Monday no less than 23,000 attended. Brown's batting matched the rather cheerless weather conditions; he took 250 minutes to score 106. His partners were in better spirits; Morris, Bradman and Harvey all scored rapidly. At the close of the first day just four wickets had fallen.

On Monday 25 wickets went down. Kent's first innings lasted 85 minutes and when the follow on was enforced they lost five more wickets for 45 runs. Evans hit out in a cavalier manner, but the game ended in two days. Todd was unable to bat due to a bruised instep, sustained when hit by a full-toss from Lindwall in his brief first innings.

KENT v AUSTRALIANS

Australians

W.A.Brown	c Evans b Ridgway	106
A.R.Morris	c Evans b Dovey	43
D.G.Bradman*	c Valentine b Crush	65
R.N.Harvey	b Ridgway	60
S.J.E.Loxton	c Valentine b Dovey	16
R.A.Hamence	c Ames b Ridgway	38
C.L.McCool	b Crush	0
I.W.Johnson	lbw b Todd	15
R.R.Lindwall	c Ames b Dovey	5
R.A.Saggers†	c Ridgway b Dovey	8
W.A.Johnston	not out	2
Extras	b 1, lb 2	3
		—
Total	(400 mins)	361

Fall of wickets: 1-64, 2-168, 3-272, 4-283, 5-295, 6-297, 7-328, 8-339, 9-353, 10-361

Kent

A.E.Fagg	b Johnston	0	b Lindwall	16
L.J.Todd	b Lindwall	0	absent injured	0
L.E.G.Ames	c Saggers b Johnston	11	c Saggers b Lindwall	6
H.A.Pawson	b Lindwall	1	c Loxton b Lindwall	35
J.G.W.Davies	not out	21	(2) c McCool b Loxton	0
B.H.Valentine*	c McCool b Johnston	0	(5) b Lindwall	5
P.Hearn	b McCool	15	(6) b Johnston	3
T.G.Evans†	b Loxton	1	(7) run out	49
E.Crush	b Loxton	0	(8) st Saggers b Johnson	1
R.R.Dovey	b McCool	0	(9) st Saggers b Johnson	2
F.Ridgway	b Loxton	0	(10) not out	5
Extras	b 1, lb 1	2	b 1, lb 1	2
		—		—
Total	(82 mins)	51	(110 mins)	124

Fall of wickets (1): 1-1, 2-11, 3-12, 4-14, 5-16, 6-48, 7-49, 8-49, 9-50, 10-51
Fall of wickets (2): 1-1, 2-20, 3-31, 4-37, 5-45, 6-116, 7-116, 8-119, 9-124

Kent Bowling

	O	M	R	W
Ridgway	41	10	119	3
Crush	15	1	82	2
Todd	17	3	51	1
Dovey	50.3	13	90	4
Davies	10	5	16	0

Australians Bowling

	O	M	R	W	O	M	R	W
Lindwall	7	1	16	2	8	1	25	4
Johnston	6	2	10	3	9	2	28	1
McCool	5	0	13	2	5	0	42	0
Loxton	5	1	10	3	6	0	12	1
Johnson					4.5	1	15	2

Umpires: A.R.Coleman and A.Lockett
Close of play: Australians 293-4 (Loxton 15, Hamence 1)

W.A.Brown scored 106 in 252 minutes with 10 fours. W.A.Brown and D.G.Bradman added 104 in 107 minutes for the 2nd wicket. W.A.Brown and R.N.Harvey added 104 in 81 minutes for the 3rd wicket. E.Crush was out 1st ball in the first innings.

GENTLEMEN v AUSTRALIANS

Played at Lord's on August 25, 26, 27 1948
Australians won by an innings and 81 runs
Toss won by Australians

Spectators flocked to the ground to see Bradman's final match at cricket's headquarters. About 18,000 were present on both first and second days. The weather and wicket were ideal for batting; Barnes failed, but Brown, Bradman and Hassett all gorged themselves. Brown played his best innings of the tour; Bradman, who hit 19 fours, threw away his wicket on reaching 150.

The declaration came when Hassett achieved 200 in the final over before lunch on the second day. Simpson and Edrich gave the Gentlemen a fair start, but afterwards the bowlers were in control. With the follow on enforced, Edrich played well, batting 195 minutes with 22 fours; he received support in the early stages from Simpson and Palmer, then Ring and Johnson dealt with the rest.

W.A.Brown scored 120 in 152 minutes with 1 five and 15 fours. D.G.Bradman scored 150 in 212 minutes with 19 fours. A.L.Hassett scored 200 in 314 minutes with 18 fours. W.A.Brown and D.G.Bradman added 181 in 199 minutes for the 2nd wicket. D.G.Bradman and A.L.Hassett added 110 in 92 minutes for the 3rd wicket. A.L.Hassett and K.R.Miller added 157 in 103 minutes for the 4th wicket. W.J.Edrich scored 128 in 195 minutes with 22 fours. W.J.Edrich and C.H.Palmer added 113 in 84 minutes for the 2nd wicket in the second innings.

GENTLEMEN v AUSTRALIANS

Australians

S.G.Barnes	c Wooller b Bailey	19
W.A.Brown	c Bailey b Wooller	120
D.G.Bradman*	c Donnelly b Brown	150
A.L.Hassett	not out	200
K.R.Miller	c Simpson b Wooller	69
S.J.E.Loxton	c Griffith b Bailey	17
R.A.Hamence	not out	24
I.W.Johnson	did not bat	
R.R.Lindwall	did not bat	
R.A.Saggers†	did not bat	
D.T.Ring	did not bat	
Extras	b 6, lb 4, w 1	11
Total	(468 mins) 5 wkts dec.	610

Fall of wickets: 1-40, 2-221, 3-331, 4-488, 5-532

Gentlemen

W.J.Edrich	b Ring	27	c Saggers b Ring		128
R.T.Simpson	c Brown b Johnson	60	c Bradman b Ring		27
C.H.Palmer	c and b Johnson	3	b Miller		29
M.P.Donnelly	lbw b Johnson	15	c Barnes b Miller		8
N.W.D.Yardley	b Miller	25	b Ring		18
F.G.Mann	lbw b Lindwall	7	c and b Ring		0
R.W.V.Robins*	b Johnson	30	b Johnson		19
W.Wooller	c Johnson b Hamence	11	c Loxton b Ring		5
T.E.Bailey	c Hamence b Ring	20	not out		14
F.R.Brown	c Hamence b Ring	18	c Brown b Johnson		17
S.C.Griffith†	not out	13	b Johnson		0
Extras	b 8, lb 8	16	b 11, lb 7, w 1		19
Total	(237 mins)	245	(265 mins)		284

Fall of wickets (1): 1-55, 2-76, 3-102, 4-121, 5-139, 6-153, 7-170, 8-210, 9-214, 10-245
Fall of wickets (2): 1-60, 2-173, 3-191, 4-217, 5-217, 6-228, 7-240, 8-260, 9-284, 10-284

Gentlemen Bowling

	O	M	R	W	
Bailey	27	4	112	2	
Wooller	24	1	131	2	
Palmer	21	3	58	0	
Edrich	16	3	49	0	
Yardley	24	5	88	0	
Brown	27	0	121	1	(1w)
Robins	4	0	22	0	
Donnelly	6	0	18	0	

Australians Bowling

	O	M	R	W	O	M	R	W	
Lindwall	13	3	39	1					
Miller	7	3	18	1	19	6	58	2	
Hamence	8	2	23	1	3	1	18	0	
Loxton	8	2	11	0	13	7	26	0	
Ring	25.3	7	74	3	32	8	70	5	(1w)
Johnson	23	7	60	4	28.5	9	69	3	
Barnes	3	2	4	0	5	0	24	0	

Umpires: P.T.Mills and J.A.Smart
Close of play: 1st day: Australians 478-3 (Hassett 119, Miller 59); 2nd day: Gentlemen (1) 237-9 (Brown 10, Griffith 13)

SOMERSET v AUSTRALIANS

Played at Taunton on August 28, 30 1948
Australians won by an innings and 374 runs
Toss won by Australians

Another county match finished in two days by an innings. This game proceeded in a very similar fashion to the last three, only Somerset proved even weaker.

On the first day the tourists hit 560 for five. Brown was run out in the first over; Barnes retired with cramp in his side with the score on 69 for one; then Hassett, Harvey, Hamence and Johnson took command. Harvey's innings was quite exceptional. He hit 2 sixes and 14 fours in batting 150 minutes. Johnson hit a maiden first-class hundred. Hassett's three figures came on his birthday.

The Monday was simply a procession of batsmen. The two Somerset innings occupied four hours and the whole was complete by tea time. The crumbling wicket gave much help to McCool and Johnson. The latter took three wickets in four balls: he took the final two wickets of the first innings with successive balls and then removed Gimblett with the second ball he bowled in the second innings.

SOMERSET v AUSTRALIANS

Australians

S.G.Barnes	retired ill	42
W.A.Brown	run out	0
A.L.Hassett*	c Watts b Redman	103
R.N.Harvey	c Luckes b Redman	126
R.A.Hamence	st Luckes b Coope	99
C.L.McCool	c Buse b Redman	6
I.W.Johnson	not out	113
K.R.Miller	not out	37
W.A.Johnston	did not bat	
R.A.Saggers†	did not bat	
D.T.Ring	did not bat	
Extras	b 7, lb 21, w 1, nb 5	34
Total	(360 mins) 5 wkts dec.	560

Fall of wickets: 1-0, 2-256, 3-298, 4-306, 5-501

Somerset

H.Gimblett	c McCool b Johnston	19	lbw b Johnston		0
M.M.Walford	st Saggers b McCool	26	c Barnes b McCool		21
H.E.Watts	st Saggers b Johnson	10	c Hassett b Miller		0
H.T.F.Buse	c Hamence b McCool	4	c McCool b Johnston		21
G.E.S.Woodhouse*	not out	33	b Johnston		3
M.Coope	b Ring	2	c Hamence b McCool		8
M.F.Tremlett	b McCool	0	c Miller b McCool		2
A.W.Wellard	c Ring b McCool	0	c Johnston b McCool		5
W.T.Luckes†	lbw b Ring	5	not out		1
J.Redman	c Hassett b Johnston	8	c Ring b Johnston		5
H.L.Hazell	b Johnston	0	lbw b Johnston		0
Extras	b 4, lb 4	8	b 4, lb 1		5
Total	(125 mins)	115	(98 mins)		71

Fall of wickets (1): 1-31, 2-50, 3-63, 4-64, 5-67, 6-68, 7-68, 8-84, 9-115, 10-115
Fall of wickets (2): 1-0, 2-1, 3-35, 4-49, 5-57, 6-58, 7-65, 8-66, 9-71, 10-71

Somerset Bowling

	O	M	R	W	
Wellard	25	2	103	0	
Tremlett	21	0	106	0	(4nb)
Hazell	27	3	114	0	
Buse	27	4	88	0	(1nb)
Coope	6	0	37	1	
Redman	16	3	78	3	(1w)

Australians Bowling

	O	M	R	W	O	M	R	W
Miller	5	1	20	0	3	1	5	1
Johnston	11.5	3	34	3	17.4	9	34	5
Johnson	9	5	15	1	1	0	4	0
McCool	11	0	21	4	14	4	23	4
Ring	9	4	17	2				

Umpires: F.S.Lee and D.Hendren
Close of play: Australians 560-5 (Johnson 113, Miller 37)

A.L.Hassett scored 103 in 175 minutes with 7 fours. R.N.Harvey scored 126 in 149 minutes with 2 sixes and 14 fours. I.W.Johnson scored 113 in 140 minutes with 2 sixes and 10 fours. A.L.Hassett and R.N.Harvey added 187 in 123 minutes for their part of the 2nd wicket partnership. R.A.Hamence and I.W.Johnson added 195 in 112 minutes for the 5th wicket. A.W.Wellard was out 1st ball in the first innings. H.L.Hazell was out 1st ball in the first innings and 2nd ball in the second innings.

SOUTH OF ENGLAND v AUSTRALIANS

Played at Hastings on September 1, 2, 3 1948
Match drawn
Toss won by Australians

The opening batsmen failed, but as at Taunton numbers 3, 4 and 5 soon made up for any earlier shortcomings. Barnes was caught behind off the first ball of the match. This brought in Bradman; his innings was flawless and contained a six and 17 fours. Harvey reached his hundred in 95 minutes. In 110 minutes 175 came for the fourth wicket.

Bradman declared at lunch on the second day. Barnett and Edrich made a very brisk start, the pair adding 78 for the first wicket in less than an hour. Barnett's 35 included a six and 5 fours. Rain stopped play soon after tea.

The third day was ruined by frequent showers; Compton batted well for his 82. With nothing to play for Hassett, Harvey and Brown came on to bowl, the last named ending with a flattering analysis.

SOUTH OF ENGLAND v AUSTRALIANS

Australians

S.G.Barnes	c Griffith b Bailey	0
W.A.Brown	c Edrich b Mallett	13
D.G.Bradman*	c Mann b Bailey	143
A.L.Hassett	c Mallett b Perks	151
R.N.Harvey	c Griffith b Perks	110
R.A.Hamence	lbw b Mallett	7
S.J.E.Loxton	not out	67
C.L.McCool	b Perks	5
R.R.Lindwall	not out	17
D.Tallon†	did not bat	
W.A.Johnston	did not bat	
Extras	b 2, lb 6, nb 1	9
Total	7 wkts dec.	522

Fall of wickets: 1-0, 2-49, 3-237, 4-412, 5-427, 6-446, 7-461

South of England

C.J.Barnett	c Hassett b Loxton	35
W.J.Edrich	c Harvey b Johnston	52
G.H.G.Doggart	c Tallon b Lindwall	8
D.C.S.Compton	c Brown b McCool	82
T.E.Bailey	c Lindwall b Harvey	25
F.G.Mann	c Loxton b Brown	31
B.H.Valentine*	c Tallon b Brown	25
S.C.Griffith†	b McCool	11
A.W.H.Mallett	c Harvey b Brown	1
R.T.D.Perks	c Tallon b Brown	10
C.Cook	not out	0
Extras	b 13, lb 2, w 3	18
Total	(257 mins)	298

Fall of wickets: 1-78, 2-98, 3-119, 4-208, 5-214, 6-270, 7-274, 8-277, 9-298, 10-298

South of England Bowling

	O	M	R	W	
Bailey	21	0	125	2	
Perks	26	5	92	3	(1nb)
Mallett	35	5	102	2	
Cook	31	5	97	0	
Compton	7	0	43	0	
Edrich	8	0	37	0	
Barnett	3	0	17	0	

Australians Bowling

	O	M	R	W	
Lindwall	10	1	45	1	
Johnston	17	3	63	1	(2w)
Loxton	11	2	17	1	(1w)
McCool	36	9	89	2	
Hamence	3	0	7	0	
Hassett	6	0	28	0	
Harvey	6	2	15	1	
Brown	4.1	0	16	4	

Umpires: F.Chester and E.Cooke
Close of play: 1st day Australians 406-3 (Hassett 136, Harvey 105); 2nd day: South of England 140-3 (Compton 27, Bailey 6)

D.G.Bradman scored 143 in 189 minutes with 1 six and 17 fours. A.L.Hassett scored 151 in 318 minutes with 19 fours. R.N.Harvey scored 100 in 95 minutes with 13 fours. D.G.Bradman and A.L.Hassett added 188 in 153 minutes for the 3rd wicket. A.L.Hassett and R.N.Harvey added 175 in 110 minutes for the 4th wicket.

H.D.G.LEVESON-GOWER'S XI v AUSTRALIANS

Played at Scarborough on September 8, 9, 10 1948
Match drawn
Toss won by H.D.G.Leveson-Gower's XI

After the defeat of the 1938 Australian tourists by Leveson-Gower's XI, it was agreed that the home side should not include more than six current England players. The Australians lost the toss, but with Hutton dismissed off the fourth ball of the match this caused them few headaches. Rain came to the rescue and further delayed the start of the second day's play.

Lindwall soon caused trouble and the rather modest batting line-up fell to pieces. The Australians found few problems with the bowling. Barnes and Morris had a hundred on the board for the first wicket. Barnes went on to score 151 in 4 hours and 31 minutes with 4 sixes and 15 fours. Bradman was in 194 minutes and then gave away his wicket. Loxton hit a ball from Brown on to his face and retired with a broken nose. The innings was declared closed after tea on the third day and the last stage of the game was not too serious. Bradman marked his farewell to English first-class cricket by bowling the last over.

S.G.Barnes scored 151 in 271 minutes with 4 sixes and 15 fours. D.G.Bradman scored 153 in 194 minutes with 2 sixes and 19 fours. S.G.Barnes and A.R.Morris added 102 in 116 minutes for the 1st wicket. S.G.Barnes and D.G.Bradman added 225 in 156 minutes for the 2nd wicket.

H.D.G.LEVESON-GOWER'S XI v AUSTRALIANS

H.D.G.Leveson-Gower's XI

L.Hutton	b Lindwall	0	lbw b Johnson		27
L.B.Fishlock	c Harvey b Johnson	38	c Morris b Johnson		26
W.J.Edrich	b Johnston	15	not out		20
M.P.Donnelly	c Miller b Johnson	36	not out		2
N.W.D.Yardley	b Johnson	34			
R.W.V.Robins*	b Lindwall	7			
F.R.Brown	c Johnson b Lindwall	0			
T.G.Evans†	b Lindwall	0			
A.V.Bedser	b Lindwall	23			
J.C.Laker	c Johnson b Lindwall	7			
T.L.Pritchard	not out	4			
Extras	b 7, lb 6	13			
Total	(211 mins)	177	(71 mins) 2 wkts		75

Fall of wickets (1): 1-0, 2-25, 3-94, 4-94, 5-113, 6-121, 7-121, 8-157, 9-168, 10-177
Fall of wickets (2): 1-46, 2-65

Australians

S.G.Barnes	c Yardley b Laker	151
A.R.Morris	b Yardley	62
D.G.Bradman*	c Hutton b Bedser	153
S.J.E.Loxton	retired hurt	12
R.N.Harvey	b Brown	23
R.R.Lindwall	c Evans b Brown	5
K.R.Miller	c Evans b Bedser	1
I.W.Johnson	c Hutton b Brown	38
D.Tallon†	c Edrich b Bedser	2
A.L.Hassett	not out	7
W.A.Johnston	not out	26
Extras	lb 7, w 1, nb 1	9
Total	(362 mins) 8 wkts dec.	489

Fall of wickets: 1-102, 2-327, 3-407, 4-412, 5-413, 6-431, 7-435, 8-459

Australians Bowling

	O	M	R	W	O	M	R	W
Lindwall	25.3	10	59	6	2	0	11	0
Johnston	13	3	20	1	2	0	9	0
Miller	8	0	28	0				
Loxton	5	2	12	0				
Johnson	15	5	45	3	7	4	12	2
Harvey					4	1	14	0
Hassett					4	0	12	0
Morris					6	1	15	0
Bradman					1	0	2	0

H.D.G.Leveson-Gower's XI Bowling

	O	M	R	W	
Pritchard	19	4	60	0	(1nb)
Bedser	27	7	72	3	
Laker	20	4	95	1	
Brown	40	4	171	3	
Robins	3	1	9	0	
Yardley	13	2	56	1	(1w)
Edrich	3	0	17	0	

Umpires: H.G.Baldwin and A.R.Coleman
Close of play: 1st day: H.D.G.Leveson-Gower's XI (1) 94-2 (Fishlock 38, Donnelly 36); 2nd day: Australians 140-1 (Barnes 47, Bradman 30)

SCOTLAND v AUSTRALIANS†

Played at Edinburgh on September 13, 14 1948
Australians won by an innings and 40 runs
Toss won by Australians

There was never any likelihood of Scotland putting up serious opposition to the Australians, though only Morris and McCool batted with any success on the first day. Laidlaw returned a well deserved set of figures for the home country.

The Scottish first innings lasted only two hours with Johnston and Johnson picking up cheap wickets. In the follow on, the non-bowlers were mainly in evidence and Morris came out with a notable analysis, after Willatt and Crosskey had given a hint of some more robust opposition which failed to materialise.

SCOTLAND v AUSTRALIANS†

Australians

S.G.Barnes	lbw b Youngson	5
A.R.Morris	b Laidlaw	112
K.R.Miller	c Wykes b Colledge	6
D.G.Bradman*	b Nicol	27
R.A.Hamence	c Laidlaw b Nicol	6
C.L.McCool	lbw b Laidlaw	52
I.W.Johnson	st Wykes b Laidlaw	0
D.Tallon	c Laidlaw b Edward	6
R.A.Saggers†	st Wykes b Laidlaw	8
D.T.Ring	not out	3
W.A.Johnston	c Wykes b Laidlaw	0
Extras	b 7, lb 4	11
Total		236

Fall of wickets: 1-18, 2-29, 3-77, 4-91, 5-200, 6-200, 7-215, 8-223, 9-236, 10-236

Scotland

G.L.Willatt	st Saggers b Johnson	6	c Saggers b Morris		25
T.R.Crosskey	c Barnes b Johnston	5	c and b Ring		36
J.C.Wykes†	c Ring b Johnston	5	st Saggers b Ring		1
I.J.M.Lumsden	st Saggers b McCool	12	b Ring		2
W.Nicol	b Johnson	1	lbw b Ring		0
B.G.W.Atkinson	c and b Johnson	16	b Morris		9
J.Aitchison	not out	25	b Morris		5
W.A.Edward	lbw b Johnston	3	not out		17
W.K.Laidlaw*	b Johnston	2	lbw b Morris		0
F.Colledge	c Saggers b Johnston	0	st Saggers b Morris		0
G.W.Youngson	b Johnston	0	st Saggers b McCool		2
Extras	b 4, lb 6	10	b 9, lb 4, nb 1		14
Total		85			111

Fall of wickets (1): 1-6, 2-22, 3-34, 4-34, 5-41, 6-63, 7-81, 8-85, 9-85, 10-85
Fall of wickets (2): 1-51, 2-63, 3-69, 4-71, 5-82, 6-83, 7-92, 8-92, 9-92, 10-111

Scotland Bowling

	O	M	R	W
Youngson	21	2	62	1
Colledge	13	2	38	1
Nicol	17	1	55	2
Edward	13	4	19	1
Laidlaw	12.2	1	51	5

Australians Bowling

	O	M	R	W	O	M	R	W	
Miller	6	3	14	0	4	1	4	0	(1nb)
Johnston	12.5	4	15	6	4	1	3	0	
Johnson	12	7	18	3	5	3	8	0	
McCool	9	4	19	1	5.3	1	20	1	
Ring	5	1	9	0	10	2	20	4	
Hamence					5	1	13	0	
Tallon					8	3	10	0	
Morris					5	1	10	5	
Barnes					9	7	9	0	

Umpires: G.W.Lawson and R.Hollingdale
Close of play: Australians all out

A.R.Morris scored 112 in 195 minutes with 9 fours. A.R.Morris and C.L.McCool added 109 in 68 minutes for the 5th wicket.

SCOTLAND v AUSTRALIANS†

Played at Aberdeen on September 17, 18 1948
Australians won by an innings and 87 runs
Toss won by Australians

The tour ended with another record crowd, about 10,000 attending on the first day. Bradman put Scotland in; as in the previous game a fair start was allowed to dwindle away. Bradman marked his final innings of the tour with another hundred and in all hit 2 sixes and 17 fours. McCool and Johnson also enjoyed themselves.

Willatt batted well in Scotland's second innings but after Ring and Johnston had made the initial inroads, Johnson took over as wicketkeeper and even Tallon picked up two wickets as Scotland subsided to another innings defeat.

SCOTLAND v AUSTRALIANS†

Scotland

G.L.Willatt	b Johnston	16	b Ring	52
T.R.Crosskey	c Ring b Morris	49	b Ring	14
J.C.Wykes†	b Morris	11	c Ring b Johnston	10
I.J.M.Lumsden	c Johnson b Morris	1	b Brown	16
W.Nicol	lbw b McCool	37	c McCool b Tallon	1
J.Aitchison	c Lindwall b McCool	32	c Brown b Tallon	9
B.G.W.Atkinson	lbw b Johnson	1	b Harvey	11
W.A.Edward	b McCool	5	lbw b Ring	0
W.K.Laidlaw*	lbw b Johnson	5	st Johnson b Ring	6
F.Colledge	b Johnson	1	b Harvey	8
G.W.Youngson	not out	5	not out	2
Extras	b 14, nb 1	15	b 12, nb 1	13
Total		178		142

Fall of wickets (1): 1-63, 2-84, 3-86, 4-91, 5-156, 6-157, 7-167, 8-168, 9-169, 10-178
Fall of wickets (2): 1-33, 2-50, 3-70, 4-71, 5-100, 6-126, 7-126, 8-126, 9-134, 10-142

Australians

C.L.McCool	c Lumsden b Edward	108
R.A.Hamence	lbw b Colledge	15
R.N.Harvey	c Aitchison b Youngson	4
R.R.Lindwall	b Laidlaw	15
I.W.Johnson	c Crosskey b Youngson	95
D.G.Bradman*	not out	123
A.R.Morris	c Aitchison b Youngson	10
W.A.Brown	not out	24
W.A.Johnston	did not bat	
D.T.Ring	did not bat	
D.Tallon†	did not bat	
Extars	b 10, lb 2, nb 1	13
Total	6 wkts dec.	407

Fall of wickets: 1-46, 2-53, 3-96, 4-188, 5-326, 6-355

Australians Bowling

	O	M	R	W		O	M	R	W	
Lindwall	10	5	12	0		4	0	16	0	
Johnston	13	4	35	1		4	0	13	1	
Ring	14	4	42	0	(1nb)	10	1	30	4	(1nb)
Johnson	20.2	11	26	3		3	0	6	0	
Morris	9	1	17	3		4	1	8	0	
McCool	16	2	31	3		7	1	19	0	
Brown						5	0	9	1	
Tallon						9	3	15	2	
Harvey						5	0	13	2	

Scotland Bowling

	O	M	R	W	
Youngson	35	3	114	3	
Colledge	27	4	93	1	
Laidlaw	10	0	62	1	(1nb)
Nicol	15	5	56	0	
Edward	18	5	69	1	

Umpires: L.E.Tyson and W.Nelson
Close of play: Australians 96-3 (McCool 54, Johnson 0)

C.L.McCool scored 108 in 180 minutes with 13 fours. D.G.Bradman scored 123 in 89 minutes with 2 sixes and 17 fours.

Test Match Averages

Played 5; Australia won 4; 1 drawn

Australia Batting and Fielding

	M	I	No	HS	Runs	Ave	100	50	Ct/St
Morris	5	9	1	196	696	87.00	3	3	4
Barnes	4	6	2	141	329	82.25	1	3	1
Bradman	5	9	2	173*	508	72.57	2	1	2
Harvey	2	3	1	112	133	66.50	1	-	3
Toshack	4	4	3	20*	51	51.00	-	-	-
Loxton	3	3	0	93	144	48.00	-	1	-
Hassett	5	8	1	137	310	44.28	1	-	6
Lindwall	5	6	0	77	191	31.83	-	1	3
Tallon	4	4	0	53	112	28.00	-	1	12/-
Miller	5	7	0	74	184	26.28	-	2	8
Brown	2	3	0	32	73	24.33	-	-	2
Johnston	5	5	2	29	62	20.66	-	-	2
Johnson	4	6	1	21	51	10.20	-	-	5
Ring	1	1	0	9	9	9.00	-	-	-
Saggers	1	1	0	5	5	5.00	-	-	2/-

Australia Bowling

	O	M	R	W	Ave	BB	5I	10M
Lindwall	222.5	57	530	27	19.62	6-20	2	-
Miller	138.1	43	301	13	23.15	4-125	-	-
Johnston	309.2	92	630	27	23.33	5-36	1	-
Toshack	173.1	70	364	11	33.09	5-40	1	-
Ring	28	13	44	1	44.00	1-44	-	-
Loxton	63	11	148	3	49.33	3-55	-	-
Johnson	183	60	427	7	61.00	3-72	-	-
Barnes	5	2	11	0				
Morris	8	1	24	0				

England Batting and Fielding

	M	I	NO	HS	Runs	Ave	100	50	Ct/St
D.C.S.Compton	5	10	1	184	562	62.44	2	2	2
C.Washbrook	4	8	1	143	356	50.85	1	2	3
L.Hutton	4	8	0	81	342	42.75	-	4	4
W.J.Edrich	5	10	0	111	319	31.90	1	2	5
T.G.Evans	5	9	2	50	188	26.85	-	-	8/4
J.C.Laker	3	6	1	63	114	22.80	-	1	-
A.V.Bedser	5	9	1	79	176	22.00	-	1	1
J.Hardstaff	1	2	0	43	43	21.50	-	-	-
J.F.Crapp	3	6	1	37	88	17.60	-	-	6
D.V.P.Wright	1	2	1	13*	17	17.00	-	-	-
N.W.D.Yardley	5	9	0	44	150	16.66	-	-	1
H.E.Dollery	2	3	0	37	38	12.66	-	-	-
A.Coxon	1	2	0	19	19	9.50	-	-	-
C.J.Barnett	1	2	0	8	14	7.00	-	-	-
J.A.Young	3	5	2	9	17	5.66	-	-	2
J.G.Dewes	1	2	0	10	11	5.50	-	-	-
K.Cranston	1	2	0	10	10	5.00	-	-	2
G.M.Emmett	1	2	0	10	10	5.00	-	-	-
R.Pollard	2	2	1	3	3	3.00	-	-	1
A.J.Watkins	1	2	0	2	2	1.00	-	-	-
W.E.Hollies	1	2	1	0*	0	0.00	-	-	-

England Bowling

	O	M	R	W	Ave	BB	5I	10M
Yardley	84	22	204	9	22.66	2-32	-	-
Hollies	56	14	131	5	26.20	5-131	1	-
Bedser	274.3	75	688	18	38.22	4-81	-	-
Pollard	102	29	218	5	43.60	3-53	-	-
Laker	155.2	42	472	9	52.44	4-138	-	-
Coxon	63	13	172	3	57.33	2-90	-	-
Young	156	64	292	5	58.40	2-118	-	-
Wright	40.3	12	123	2	61.50	1-54	-	-
Cranston	21.1	1	79	1	79.00	1-28	-	-
Edrich	53	4	238	3	79.33	1-27	-	-
Compton	37	6	156	1	156.00	1-82	-	-
Barnett	17	5	36	0				
Hutton	4	1	30	0				
Watkins	4	1	19	0				

Australian Averages in First-Class Matches In England

Played 31; won 23; lost 0; drawn 8

Batting and Fielding

	M	I	NO	HS	Runs	Ave	100	50	Ct/St
Bradman	23	31	4	187	2428	89.92	11	8	11
Hassett	22	27	6	200*	1563	74.42	7	4	23
Morris	21	29	2	290	1922	71.18	7	7	10
Brown	22	26	1	200	1448	57.92	8	1	16
Loxton	22	22	5	159*	973	57.23	3	5	13
Barnes	21	27	3	176	1354	56.41	3	8	19
Harvey	22	27	6	126	1129	53.76	4	5	17
Miller	22	26	3	202*	1088	47.30	2	8	20
Hamence	19	22	4	99	582	32.33	-	2	9
Johnson	22	22	4	113*	543	30.16	1	2	23
Tallon	14	13	2	53	283	25.72	-	2	29/14
Lindwall	22	20	3	77	411	24.17	-	2	14
Saggers	17	12	3	104*	209	23.22	1	-	23/20
McCool	17	18	3	76	306	20.40	-	3	20
Johnston	21	18	8	29	188	18.80	-	-	9
Ring	19	14	5	53	150	16.66	-	1	12
Toshack	15	12	3	20*	78	8.66	-	-	2
Substitute									3

Bowling

	O	M	R	W	Ave	BB	5I	10M
Brown	4.1	0	16	4	4.00	4-16	-	-
Lindwall	573.4	139	1349	86	15.68	6-14	6	1
Johnston	850.1	279	1675	102	16.42	6-18	6	2
Miller	429.4	117	985	56	17.58	6-42	3	-
McCool	399.4	98	1016	57	17.82	7-78	3	-
Johnson	668	228	1562	85	18.37	7-42	5	1
Toshack	502	172	1056	50	21.12	7-81	4	-
Hamence	56.3	13	150	7	21.42	2-13	-	-
Loxton	361.2	92	695	32	21.71	3-10	-	-
Ring	542.4	155	1309	60	21.81	5-45	3	-
Harvey	10	3	29	1	29.00	1-15	-	-
Morris	35	9	91	2	45.50	1-6	-	-
Barnes	65.4	26	121	2	60.50	1-11	-	-
Bradman	1	0	2	0				
Hassett	12	0	48	0				

The following 55 centuries were scored by the Australian team in all matches:

290	A.R.Morris	v Gloucestershire		126	R.N.Harvey	v Somerset
202*	K.R.Miller	v Leicestershire		123*	I.W.Johnson	v Scotland†
200*	A.L.Hassett	v Gentlemen		123	S.J.E.Loxton	v Middlesex
200	W.A.Brown	v Cambridge University		122	W.A.Brown	v Nottinghamshire
196	A.R.Morris	v England (5th Test)		120	S.J.E.Loxton	v Essex
187	D.G.Bradman	v Essex		120	W.A.Brown	v Gentlemen
184	A.R.Morris	v Sussex		115	A.R.Morris	v Western Australia
182	A.R.Morris	v England (4th Test)		115	D.G.Bradman	v Western Australia
176	S.G.Barnes	v Surrey		113*	I.W.Johnson	v Somerset
173*	D.G.Bradman	v England (4th Test)		113	W.A.Brown	v Yorkshire
163	K.R.Miller	v M.C.C.		112	R.N.Harvey	v England (4th Test)
159*	S.J.E.Loxton	v Gloucestershire		112	A.R.Morris	v Scotland†
153	W.A.Brown	v Essex		111	S.G.Barnes	v Tasmania†
153	D.G.Bradman	v H.D.G.Leveson-Gower's XI		110	A.L.Hassett	v Surrey
151	A.L.Hassett	v South of England		110	R.N.Harvey	v South of England
151	S.G.Barnes	v H.D.G.Leveson-Gower's XI		109	D.G.Bradman	v Sussex
150	D.G.Bradman	v Gentlemen		109	A.R.Morris	v Middlesex
146	D.G.Bradman	v Surrey		108	W.A.Brown	v Oxford University
143	D.G.Bradman	v South of England		108	C.L.McCool	v Scotland†
141	S.G.Barnes	v England (2nd Test)		107	D.G.Bradman	v Worcestershire
140	W.A.Brown	v Derbyshire		106	W.A.Brown	v Kent
139	A.L.Hassett	v Surrey		105	A.R.Morris	v England (2nd Test)
138	A.R.Morris	v Worcestershire		104	R.N.Harvey	v Tasmania†
138	D.G.Bradman	v England (1st Test)		104	R.A.Saggers	v Essex
137	A.L.Hassett	v England (1st Test)		103	A.L.Hassett	v Somerset
133*	D.G.Bradman	v Lancashire		100*	R.N.Harvey	v Sussex
128	D.G.Bradman	v Surrey		100	A.L.Hassett	v Tasmania†
127	A.L.Hassett	v Northamptonshire				

Australian Averages in All Matches In England

Played 34; won 25; lost 0; drawn 9

Batting and Fielding

	M	I	NO	HS	Runs	Ave	100	50	Ct/St
Bradman	25	33	5	187	2578	92.07	12	8	11
Hassett	23	28	6	200*	1566	71.18	7	4	24
Morris	23	31	2	290	2044	70.48	8	7	10
Brown	24	28	2	200	1521	58.50	8	1	17
Loxton	23	23	5	159*	988	54.88	3	5	13
Barnes	22	28	3	176	1359	54.36	3	8	20
Harvey	24	29	6	126	1135	49.34	4	5	17
Miller	24	28	3	202*	1149	45.96	2	8	20
Johnson	25	25	4	113*	682	32.47	1	3	25/1
Hamence	22	25	4	99	627	29.85	-	2	9
McCool	20	21	3	108	530	29.44	1	5	21
Lindwall	23	21	3	77	426	23.66	-	2	15
Tallon	17	15	2	53	290	22.30	-	2	29/14
Saggers	19	14	3	104*	239	21.72	1	-	25/27
Ring	22	16	7	53	154	17.11	-	1	16
Johnston	23	19	8	29	188	17.09	-	-	9
Toshack	15	12	3	20*	78	8.66	-	-	2
Substitute									3

Bowling

	O	M	R	W	Ave	BB	5I	10M
Brown	9.1	1	25	5	5.00	4-16	-	-
Tallon	9	3	15	2	7.50	2-15	-	-
Morris	53	12	126	10	12.60	5-10	1	-
Harvey	15	3	42	3	14.00	2-13	-	-
Johnston	884	288	1741	110	15.82	6-15	7	2
Lindwall	587.4	144	1377	86	16.01	6-14	6	1
Johnson	714.2	250	1622	92	17.63	7-42	5	1
McCool	446.1	110	1122	63	17.80	7-78	3	-
Miller	447.4	124	1020	57	17.89	6-42	3	-
Ring	588.4	165	1434	69	20.78	5-45	3	-
Toshack	502	172	1056	50	21.12	7-81	4	-
Loxton	367.2	95	703	33	21.30	3-10	-	-
Hamence	61.3	14	163	7	23.28	2-13	-	-
Barnes	74.4	33	130	2	65.00	1-11	-	-
Bradman	1	0	2	0				
Hassett	12	0	48	0				
Tallon	8	3	10	0				

The following 8 centuries were scored against the Australian team in all matches:

184	D.C.S.Compton	England (1st Test)
145*	D.C.S.Compton	England (3rd Test)
143	C.Washbrook	England (4th Test)
128	W.J.Edrich	Gentlemen†
112	C.W.Langdon	Western Australia
111	W.J.Edrich	England (4th Test)
107	J.Hardstaff	Nottinghamshire
100*	J.F.Crapp	Gloucestershire

Australian Averages in All First-class Matches

Played 32; won 23; lost 0; drawn 9

Batting and Fielding

	M	I	NO	HS	Runs	Ave	100	50	Ct/St
Bradman	24	32	4	187	2543	90.82	12	8	11
Hassett	22	27	6	200*	1563	74.42	7	4	23
Morris	22	30	2	290	2037	72.75	8	7	10
Loxton	22	22	5	159*	973	57.23	3	5	13
Barnes	21	27	3	176	1354	56.41	3	8	19
Brown	23	27	1	200	1457	56.03	8	1	17
Harvey	23	28	6	126	1208	54.90	4	6	17
Miller	23	27	3	202*	1131	47.12	2	8	21
Hamence	20	23	5	99	615	34.16	-	2	9
Johnson	23	23	4	113*	554	29.15	1	2	24
Tallon	14	13	2	53	283	25.72	-	2	29/14
Lindwall	22	20	3	77	411	24.17	-	2	14
Saggers	18	13	4	104*	209	23.22	1	-	25/20
McCool	18	19	3	76	324	20.25	-	3	20
Johnston	22	18	8	29	188	18.80	-	-	11
Ring	19	14	5	53	150	16.66	-	1	12
Toshack	16	12	3	20*	78	8.66	-	-	2
Substitute									3

Bowling

	O	M	R	W	Ave	BB	5I	10M
Brown	4.1	0	16	4	4.00	4-16	-	-
Lindwall	573.4	139	1349	86	15.68	6-14	6	1
Johnston	875.1	282	1746	104	16.78	6-18	6	2
Miller	450.4	123	1033	59	17.50	6-42	3	-
Johnson	694	233	1643	88	18.67	7-42	5	1
McCool	423.3	99	1151	60	19.18	7-78	3	-
Hamence	56.3	13	150	7	21.42	2-13	-	-
Toshack	525	174	1118	52	21.50	7-81	4	-
Loxton	361.2	92	695	32	21.71	3-10	-	-
Ring	542.4	155	1309	60	21.81	5-45	3	-
Harvey	10	3	29	1	29.00	1-15	-	-
Morris	35	9	91	2	45.50	1-6	-	-
Barnes	65.4	26	121	2	60.50	1-11	-	-
Bradman	1	0	2	0				
Hassett	12	0	48	0				

There were 33 instances of 5 wickets in an innings for the Australian team in all matches:

7-42	I.W.Johnson	v Leicestershire		5-24	E.R.H.Toshack	v Tasmania†
7-78	C.L.McCool	v Cambridge University		5-25	K.R.Miller	v Hampshire
7-81	E.R.H.Toshack	v Yorkshire		5-25	R.R.Lindwall	v Sussex
6-14	R.R.Lindwall	v Nottinghamshire		5-31	E.R.H.Toshack	v Essex
6-15	W.A.Johnston	v Scotland†		5-32	I.W.Johnson	v Gloucestershire
6-18	W.A.Johnston	v Yorkshire		5-34	W.A.Johnston	v Somerset
6-20	R.R.Lindwall	v England (5th Test)		5-36	W.A.Johnston	v England (1st Test)
6-34	R.R.Lindwall	v Sussex		5-40	E.R.H.Toshack	v England (2nd Test)
6-37	I.W.Johnson	v Essex		5-43	W.A.Johnston	v Hampshire
6-42	K.R.Miller	v Yorkshire		5-45	D.T.Ring	v Leicestershire
6-51	E.R.H.Toshack	v M.C.C.		5-46	K.R.Miller	v Cambridge University
6-59	R.R.Lindwall	v H.D.G.Leveson-Gower's XI		5-47	D.T.Ring	v Gloucestershire
6-68	I.W.Johnson	v Gloucestershire		5-49	W.A.Johnston	v Lancashire
6-74	W.A.Johnston	v Hampshire		5-53	I.W.Johnson	v Surrey
6-77	C.L.McCool	v Derbyshire		5-70	R.R.Lindwall	v England (2nd Test)
6-113	C.L.McCool	v Surrey		5-70	D.T.Ring	v Gent;lemen
5-10	A.R.Morris	v Scotland†				

There were 4 instances of 10 wickets in a match for the Australian team in all matches:

11-59	R.R.Lindwall	v Sussex
11-100	I.W.Johnson	v Gloucestershire
11-117	W.A.Johnston	v Hampshire
10-40	W.A.Johnston	v Yorkshire

Australian Averages in All Matches

Played 38; won 26; lost 0; drawn 12

Batting and Fielding

	M	I	NO	HS	Runs	Ave	100	50	Ct/St
Bradman	28	36	5	187	2758	88.96	13	8	12
Morris	26	34	2	290	2253	70.40	9	8	11
Hassett	25	30	6	200*	1689	70.37	8	4	25
Loxton	26	26	6	159*	1142	57.10	3	7	14
Barnes	25	31	4	176	1530	56.66	4	8	22
Brown	27	31	2	200	1599	55.13	8	2	19
Harvey	28	33	6	126	1327	49.14	5	6	18
Miller	27	30	3	202*	1254	46.44	2	8	23
Johnson	28	27	5	113*	695	31.59	1	3	29/1
Hamence	24	27	5	99	660	30.00	-	2	9
McCool	22	23	3	108	580	29.00	1	5	21
Lindwall	24	22	3	77	491	25.84	-	3	15
Tallon	17	15	2	53	290	22.30	-	2	29/14
Saggers	23	17	5	104*	251	20.91	1	-	30/27
Ring	24	17	8	53	160	17.77	-	1	16
Johnston	26	20	8	29	198	16.50	-	-	12
Toshack	18	13	3	20*	78	7.80	-	-	2
Substitute									3

Bowling

	O	M	R	W	Ave	BB	5I	10M
Brown	9.1	1	25	5	5.00	4-16	-	-
Tallon	9	3	15	2	7.50	2-15	-	-
Morris	57	14	132	11	12.00	5-10	1	-
Harvey	15	3	42	3	14.00	2-13	-	-
Lindwall	602.4	145	1421	89	15.96	6-14	6	1
Johnston	937	296	1891	116	16.30	6-15	7	2
Miller	480.4	131	1108	62	17.87	6-42	3	-
Johnson	758.2	260	1760	97	18.14	7-42	5	1
McCool	485	112	1348	70	19.25	7-78	3	-
Toshack	546.2	178	1188	58	20.48	7-81	5	-
Loxton	387.2	98	758	37	20.48	3-10	-	-
Ring	599	167	1546	73	21.17	5-45	3	-
Hamence	61.3	14	163	7	23.28	2-13	-	-
Barnes	83.6	37	141	6	23.50	3-1	-	-
Bradman	1	0	2	0				
Hassett	12	0	48	0				
Tallon	8	3	10	0				

There were 11 instances of 5 wickets in an innings against the Australian team in all matches:

8-107	W.E.Hollies	Warwickshire
6-51	T.F.Smailes	Yorkshire
6-65	J.M.Sims	Middlesex
6-73	W.B.Roberts	Lancashire
6-135	P.F.Jackson	Worcestershire
5-57	C.J.Knott	Hampshire
5-57	A.E.Nutter	Northamptonshire
5-63	I.T.Clay	Tasmania†
5-76	T.K.Jackson	Durham†
5-91	V.E.Jackson	Leicestershire
5-131	W.E.Hollies	England (5th Test)

There was no instance of 10 wickets in a match against the Australian team - the best were:

9-83	T.F.Smailes	Yorkshire
9-124	W.E.Hollies	Warwickshire

The End of the Tour

For the first time an Australian touring team completed its programme of first-class matches in England without suffering a single reverse. On one hand the tourists were acclaimed as the strongest combination ever to visit England, on the other hand such critics as W.J.O'Reilly pointed out that the poor quality of the English opposition made the Australians appear better than they in reality were. O'Reilly commented:
"The Australians had a fairly hollow round of victories against a range of spent volcanoes which masqueraded under the name of England county clubs."

To the ordinary spectator however it seemed that Bradman and his side were the greatest of all time. The immense crowds surely prove that point. It is impossible to give any exact figures for the total attendance at Australian matches because county members, who comprised up to 30% of the spectators, were not normally counted as they entered the ground. However a guess would put the total at 1,250,000. The English critics, unlike O'Reilly and indeed Fingleton, regarded the Australians, by and large as the best side ever to tour England. H.S.Altham in his long and comprehensive comparison of 1948 with its predecessors notes that the batting of the present side was the best ever, with the proviso that the Australians did not have to face any genuinely fast bowlers. Altham regarded the leadership of Bradman and the general out-cricket of the team quite outstanding. He thought that Lindwall and Miller were not quite up to the standard of Gregory and McDonald and that he could not compare the spin bowling of McCool and Ring with Mailey, O'Reilly and Fleetwood-Smith, simply because McCool and Ring were required so little. However the 1948 bowling had a remarkable facet in that Miller could bowl off-breaks if required and Johnston was also two bowlers in one.

The review by R.J.Hayter in *Wisden* was equally fulsome in its praise. It is however not possible to make any accurate comparison between one generation of cricketers and another, because circumstances alter with the times. Having said that, the record of Bradman which is so far beyond any of his own contemporaries, must place him as the greatest of all batsmen and this tour provided him with a perfect backdrop for his farewell season in competitive cricket. The figures, which are the prime reason for this book, can be left to tell the detailed story of the Australians' triumph.